The Pain of Waiting

by

Louise Sibley

Dear Reader,

I don't know where to start, so perhaps the beginning would be the best place. If you're one of those Christian women that are easily offended and of a delicate disposition, then I suggest you don't read this because I'm going to write this truthfully and frankly.

My friends will tell you that I call a spade a spade, and they're right. If I was looking for a practical, straightforward, 'say it how it is' book, then I'd want to read this. I wish I could go back twenty-four years and whisper a few truths to my younger self, but obviously I can't, so instead, I hope I can whisper a few truths to you.

I have been married for twenty-four years. My husband and I are pastoring a church in East Devon and I have been a Christian since I was a young child, so this is a Christian book. If you're not a Christian and you are now groaning because you've wasted your money on some religious mumbo-jumbo, then just go to the end of the book first and try to be open minded. You're reading this because you are in the same position as thousands of other women, but I truly believe that God is the only answer to infertility and without him, I would have crumbled and died years ago.

So this is my opening invitation. Read on if you want God to help you or chuck this book in the recycling bin if you're a cynic and have given up.

Sticking with it? Good, so let's get started.

Harry

I'm the pastor's daughter. It's not always a great job to have, because people expect you to be perfect and spiritual all the time. They think that you have your life together and that everything is straightforward and easy for you because you've got the pastor and his wife as your parents, but believe me, it's harder than you think.

My parents are great people. They have been pastoring for what seems like their entire adult Christian lives, but they always had time for me and my sister, and we had a good childhood. I grew up on a farm in Devon and my dad was also a dairy farmer until he sold his farm and went into full time ministry as the leader of our church. It was at this time, at the tender age of fifteen, that I met and fell madly in love with my future husband Jon, who was twenty-one at the time. My parents were not impressed and thought he was too old for me, but when they did some digging and found out who he was and who his parents were, they were a little happier because his family was also nice, respectable Christians and my gorgeous and totally hot boyfriend was therefore deemed suitable for me; the pastor's daughter.

Fast forward a few years of dating, arguing, crying, dumping each other, dating a couple of other guys who were nowhere near as cute as Jon, and having to put up with a girl whom Jon dated on the rebound too, and I find myself engaged at the tender age of eighteen, to my lovely boyfriend on Axminster Carnival night, September 12th 1987.

Jon and I weren't the only ones to get engaged that year. My friend Michaela, and her sister Penny, also got engaged to their long-term boyfriends, and another friend of ours called Jane became engaged too. We all went to the same church and for a few months, it was wedding madness. Penny and I were bridesmaids for Michaela, and within the space of four months, all four couples were married with weddings in May, June, July, and September of 1988. Jon and I married in the July.

As soon as we were married, we started talking about babies. Actually, we'd talked about babies a long time before we got married and had decided that we wanted a big family, but we wanted to have children straight away now that we were married, so it was often a topic of conversation. I wasn't expecting to get pregnant straight away. I wasn't stupid and I knew that sometimes things took a while, so I was fine when we didn't conceive in the first few months. I was actually quite knowledgeable about conceiving babies, so I excused our lack of success with all kinds of reasons, such as Jon had a cold one month, so his sperm wasn't as healthy as they could have been, things were stressful at work for both of us so we weren't relaxed enough, and we hadn't had sex on the right days, etc., but as time went on, worry started to pick away at me and I began to suspect that there was something wrong.

My first trip to the doctor was pointless. He basically told me to go away and keep trying. He'd been my doctor since my birth, and he told me that my mother was fine, so I would be too, which wasn't exactly helpful, but I trusted him, felt reassured that I was panicking for no reason and we kept trying. We'd been married for a year now and still nothing.

But every month that I got my period, I felt so disappointed, that it started to affect my personality and before long, it had begun to consume every waking moment of my day. I couldn't think about anything else because having a baby with Jon meant everything to me and I couldn't understand why God was punishing me like this. In my eyes, I'd done everything right. I'd even managed to be a virgin when I got married, so what had I done that was so bad, and why wasn't I getting pregnant?

Jon and I prayed about getting pregnant all the time. It was the same prayer over and over again. How many different ways can you ask God for a baby? We prayed together, we prayed separately, we prayed out walking together, we prayed in the privacy of our bedroom, we prayed so much, I began to feel all prayed out. We didn't mention anything to our parents for a few months, and Jon's mum and dad began to think that we didn't want to have children because I was career-minded and at the time I work for Lloyds Bank, but I felt such a failure at not being able to produce the first grandchild, that I just couldn't bring myself to tell them the truth.

We went to a conference in Peterborough called Faith Camp, and I was prayed for by several of the guest speakers. Any chance that I got for prayer, I took it. I remember one night heading to the ladies toilets just before I went back to our tent and I was sitting on the loo and God spoke to me. It was just a very quiet thought that went around my head, but I knew it wasn't me because it didn't sound how I sound in my head. God said to me that I was childless, not infertile, and it was a revelation to me that night. There is a big difference between childlessness and infertility. Infertile means you can't have children naturally, childless means you haven't got them yet. I held onto that thought for a long time and revisited it often when I was feeling upset and disappointed.

I was working in the bank one day and a lady from our church was paying in some money. She seemed to be hanging around and waiting for me to serve her so I opened up the till and smiled at her. She leaned forward and whispered to me through the glass, asking me if she could have a private word with me after I had served her, so I said that was fine and once I had finished with her business, I closed my till and met her at the staff door.

"I've just had a word from God about you," she whispered. "I saw the word pregnant written over your head. Are you trying for a baby?"

I nodded and she promised to pray for me, but that was another word that lifted my spirit for a while.

One day, a friend of mine came looking for me and she was in a terrible state. She was sobbing and choking and I didn't know what the matter was with her, so I agreed to meet her for lunch in the pub and I phoned Jon to say that I wouldn't be home at lunchtime. We sat in the corner of the pub trying to look as inconspicuous as possible, even though her mascara was running down her chin and her eyes and nose were red and puffy and she told me that she was pregnant with her boyfriend's child and neither of them wanted it. She was twenty and he was twenty one and they'd 'accidentally' got pregnant. He wanted her to have an abortion, and together they had booked her into a clinic.

I can't begin to express how devastated I felt. I begged her to let me have her baby. I said I would help her through the pregnancy, I'd help buy extra food for her and get her some nice maternity clothes, I even said she could move in with us and I'd look after her because her boyfriend was a selfish pig, but in the end, she decided to end the pregnancy, and I went home and balled my eyes out. I promised my friend that I would be at the end of the phone after she'd had the operation and I took the day off work so that I could wait for her call. I paced the lounge knowing that somewhere only a few miles away she was having her baby removed from her womb and it made me feel physically sick. I asked God to forgive her and to give her peace about the choice that she had made, but when her phone call came, she was absolutely distraught. She immediately regretted her decision and she was so ashamed of herself, she could barely speak to me. I didn't have a clue what to say to her. I loved her as my friend, but I just couldn't find the right words to say. She'd been in a ward with other girls that were having abortions and she had heard some of them laughing afterwards whilst they were outside having a cigarette and talking about the abortion as if it was no big deal. She didn't want to be like them, laughing and relieved that it was over, she wanted to be punished for what she had done, and she couldn't find any peace whatsoever.

I've written a small chapter on abortion further on, so I'm going to leave this story for now, but the only reason I wrote this was because it was part of what I saw as the injustice of everything that was happening to me at the time.

I decided to visit my Nana who lived just around the corner from me, because I wanted to tell her everything. We'd had conversations before about sex and babies, in fact, she was the one that had asked me, just before I had got married, if I knew what a penis was. I was so horribly embarrassed that I could barely look her in the eye. She had married my Granddad not knowing how to have a baby or fully understanding the human body. She had no idea about sex and yet she had conceived my uncle during her honeymoon.

Anyway, on this particular day, I told her that I couldn't get pregnant and she wasn't very sympathetic at all. She patted my hand and told me that it would happen for me and that I wasn't to worry, and I smiled and nodded, hoping that she was right. A few months later, she died, and I was devastated that she would never see any babies that I might have in the future.

So, as a lot of people did and still do, we filled our lives with other things just because we wanted other things in our lives other than this obsession with getting pregnant. We adopted a cat. She was called Sally and she was lovely. We later found out that Jon was allergic to cats, but we still kept her and he sneezed on for the next twelve years of her life. We also adopted a dog. A stinky, rough-haired terrier called Scoobie who had a habit of chewing my shoes and burying them in the garden, and we went on expensive foreign holidays to France, Turkey and the Canary Islands because I thought that perhaps a relaxing holiday in the sun would be the perfect opportunity to conceive a child. It wasn't, but the holidays were nice.

Our lives were quite stressful, Jon's job was not very stable and he was made redundant several times so this was not conducive to being in a relaxed frame of mind. But the holidays were not the answer, neither could pets make up for not having a child. We spent a lot of money on clothes, dinners out with friends, and various other things that we hoped would make us happy and fulfilled, but nothing could replace the desire to have a baby.

I was sick to death of people giving us suggestions, like they were some kind of experts on getting pregnant. It was amazing how many people 'understood' how we were feeling, when really they were clueless and completely ignorant of our predicament. They would tell us that they had waited a long time for a baby, and when we asked them how long, they would say six months! I was never rude to them personally, but the times I wanted to yell right in their faces and tell them to shut up, was numerous. They were all well meaning, but I wished I had never listened to any of them. They drove me mad with their advice and I wanted them all to leave me alone.

The doctor had suggested that we didn't try so hard for a baby and just let things happen naturally, but my head always knew when I was supposed to be ovulating and I couldn't pretend that I didn't care if we didn't make love on the right day because we had to, or risk missing another month. You can't fool your body into not trying so hard. What a ridiculous thing to say. Your heart yearns for this child, your mind dreams of this child and your body is longing to be pregnant. How can you lie to your heart, your head and your body and say you're not so bothered this month? You are caught up in a vicious circle of pain, disappointment and loneliness. It feels like this is only happening to you. You have your period, so you're upset. You ovulate, so you're all positive and excited again because you hope that this is the month that you're going to get pregnant, then when you start getting sore boobs and water retention, and you snap at your husband for no particular reason, you hope that it's early pregnancy signs and not premenstrual signs, but then you get the cramps, your period starts and hurt spreads across your chest again. It's not going to be this month and now you have to break the news to your husband, who feels like he's let you down again. It's a horrible, vicious, heartbreaking circle and it has to end, somehow…..

We had now been trying for a baby for two and a half years, so my doctor reluctantly agreed to send me and Jon for some fertility tests at the local hospital. I got the impression that he thought I was making a fuss about nothing, and that I needed to be patient, but being patient wasn't working so we were relieved when he our doctor made a referral to a specialist. I finally felt as if we were getting the help we needed and soon everything would be sorted out. As soon as I got my 'get pregnant pill', my whole life would be complete.

We turned up at the hospital fully expecting to be given medication in a bottle which we were to take twice a day, but that never happened. Instead, we were given a stupid chart to fill in. I had to take my temperature every day for a month and then come back to see him again. Another month! Did he have any idea what another month meant? I didn't like him from the first moment I met him *and* I had to be examined by him too which was not a very pleasant experience. I had never been 'examined' before and it was horrible. I lay on my back with my legs in stirrups wondering why I was the one that had to go through this. I just wanted to curl up and hide in a corner somewhere, but instead I was being treated like a lump of meat and there was more intrusive, embarrassing examinations to come.

Ever heard of the post coital test? No? Then you're very, very blessed. Jon and I had to have sex together and then rush to the hospital within an hour of sex, so that I could be examined, *again,* by the same doctor who had already seen my undercarriage and declared it normal and healthy. I have to say that it was probably the singular, most humiliating experience of my life and one that I would never, ever wish to repeat.

Jon had to deliver a sperm sample and it was a disaster, because on the week that he had to give the sample, he got the flu and consequently his sperm got the flu too. The hospital gave us the results and told us that they couldn't find any viable sperm and that we had to come back again for more tests, in a month's time. Another month! I wanted a baby by Christmas! Didn't they know that?

Jon's second sperm test came back perfectly normal, so to our relief, he was not a Jaffa, (like a Jaffa orange that has no seeds), as one of our sensitive friends had nicely put it. But my infertility was still unexplained until one day when my ovulation results came back, and I was informed quite bluntly, that I didn't ovulate.

The last few years had been all my fault. I was the infertile one. I was the abnormal one, the 'non- ovulating woman' one, and I was responsible for all the stress that we had both endured. My body was not working properly and all they could offer me was something to stimulate ovulation, but there were no guarantees and it wasn't foolproof. The specialist at the hospital said that it didn't work for most women, but I could give it a try. Jon and I were up for trying anything and we embarked on a course of treatment which we hoped would prove the doctor wrong. IVF was not an option, we were skint; it cost thousands of pounds and there were no guarantees with that either. We didn't want to end up childless and in debt. We talked about other forms of conception, using someone else's eggs and Jon's sperm, but we felt that it wouldn't have been our genetic baby, so we decided against that route.

I was talking to Jon today, twenty four years later and asking him if he could remember how he felt at the time and what his memories were and he told me that the thing he remembers most was the overwhelming sadness and hopelessness that seemed to be part of our lives for such a long time. As a man, he felt it was his job to make everything right for me, to fix things and to make me happy, but he couldn't do anything about this and it broke his heart.

I visited my aunty one day, and I was talking things over with her, and she prayed for me, like everyone did, that I would get pregnant soon and that everything would work out for me, but in my heart, I felt as if her prayer was pointless and worthless.

"Why don't you think you're going to have children?" she suddenly asked me, as if she'd been prompted by something.

I'd remembered an incident that had happened several years before, when I was talking with my friends Penny and Michaela, and we had been talking about having children.

"I was talking with Penny and Michaela," I said. "And we were saying how awful it would be if one of us couldn't have children."

My aunty nodded as she listened to me. "And?"

"And I knew that it would be me," I said. "Out of the three of us, I just knew it would be me."

My aunty prayed for me again after I had confessed this to her, but I can't remember how she prayed or what she said. I was too preoccupied with the fact that my greatest fear had come true and now I was doomed to live a life without children because I'd cursed myself. I would never know what it was like to be pregnant. I would never hold my husband's newborn child in my arms, and I would never be anyone's mummy. I had let my husband down. I had let my parents and parents-in-law down and I was a failure as a woman. In my lowest moments, I would cry and sometimes blame everything on Jon, even though there was nothing wrong with his baby making equipment. I would tell him that he should divorce me and find a woman that could have his children because there was no point in being with me anymore. It was all down to me and the fact that I didn't ovulate. I felt unfeminine, ugly, worthless, pointless, and bitter. Anger and jealousy were firmly rooted in my heart and I didn't want to be sociable with anyone.

One day I was watching the television, and there happened to be a programme on the television called 'Find me a Family'. It was an adoption programme, featuring various children that needed a 'forever family', and I was definitely interested. I talked it over with Jon and he agreed to speak to a couple of social workers from the adoption team at our local social services office. They arrived at our house and I was very excited, feeling that perhaps this was God's idea for us all along and that we were finally going to have the baby that we so desperately wanted. They sat and had a cup of tea and basically told us no. We were in the middle of fertility treatment, and young, so we were likely to have our own children soon and it wasn't the right time for us. I couldn't believe that they didn't want us. I told them all about the programme that I had watched and how desperate they were for adoptive parents and they just smiled, nodded, agreed with everything I had said…. and they still said no. I felt like I was in a daze when they left. They told us that if we still wanted to consider adoption in a couple of years when fertility treatment hadn't worked, then to contact them again, but for now, it was another no.

But I wasn't giving up on making my family happen. I changed tack and started thinking about fostering instead of adopting. I knew a couple that had fostered a child and had gone on to adopt that child, so I considered it a back door into adoption. The only people we knew that were fostering children, were friends of ours from Hemyock, Glyn and Shirley, but we hadn't spoken to them in months and so completely out of the blue, they received a phone call from us and agreed to meet us at their local pub to chat about fostering.

Glyn and Shirley were fostering teenage boys, four of them in fact, aged fifteen, fifteen, sixteen and seventeen and they were exhausted and in need of some time out. To our surprise, they asked us to consider stepping into their shoes and fostering the four boys in their huge farmhouse in Hemyock and fostering as a full time job for both of us. They asked us to go home and pray about it, which we did, and within a few days, we had decided to take up the challenge. We all contacted social services to tell them what our plans were and I think because SS were disappointed to be losing Glyn and Shirley as foster parents, they were also relieved that the boys were still going to continue living where they were, albeit with new carers, so they agreed to start the approval process. We went through a lengthy approval and at the tender age of twenty-two, I was approved, along with Jon, who was now twenty eight, to foster the four teenage boys and pretend that we were their parents, even though I was only five years older than the oldest one.

It was a very 'interesting' experience and one that I was no where near ready to tackle. Jon had worked as a residential social worker in a children's home in the town where we lived, so he had a good idea of what to expect. I was completely naïve and stupid about the job we had just taken on and the boys knew it. On our first night, they invited all their friends to tea, just to suss us out, and I ended up cooking fish fingers, chips and beans for eleven teenagers, even though my cooking skills were pretty appalling. I even managed to burn coleslaw once, but that's another story. I can't honestly say that the good times outweighed the bad, because for me, they didn't. I often escaped to my mum's house or Michaela's house for the weekend because I just hated the job. There were times that were fun and we laughed a lot, but the boys never took me seriously, and it was a struggle to maintain any kind of control in a house that was so full of testosterone. Most of the time I wanted to cry. We were still trying for a baby, but I was a walking stress bomb and nothing happened. One of the lads that we fostered was very violent and aggressive and he really hated me. He rummaged through our things when we were out one day, and found photographs of me getting dressed for my wedding and I was only wearing my lingerie. My sister had taken the photo as a joke and stupidly, I'd kept the photo. The next thing I knew, the photo had been pinned to the village notice board by this lad, for everyone in the village to see and I was humiliated beyond belief. It was the last straw. My ridiculous, fantasies about fostering children to make my family happen, were not happening and I was still miserable. Our entire income depended on fostering the boys because both of us had given up our jobs to move in and look after them full time. We were not given any support, as promised by the local church or by social services, and we were isolated in a rural village with no family living near us. It was another desperate time for me in particular, but Jon coped much better and was much more stoic than me. I just wanted out.

Then out of the blue, my sister became pregnant and I was absolutely distraught. It was a shock, first and foremost, but I physically felt as if I had been punched in the stomach. I remember Jon holding me up, walking me to the car and driving me home from my parents house because I was stunned at the injustice of it all. Usually, I was very good at putting on a happy face in front of most people and I could even manage to say the right words of congratulations when necessary, but this time, because it was my sister, inside I was dying, and my poor husband had to continually pick up the shattered pieces of me, as I crumbled every time one of our friends had a baby.

My beautiful niece Laura, was born in October 1991. She was so cute and cuddly, and I loved her straight away. She was the first grandchild to be born in our family. Everyone was thrilled and I was genuinely happy for my sister, however a few weeks after Laura's birth, my dad started getting a lot of chest pain and he developed a chest infection that didn't respond to normal antibiotics. Eventually he was admitted to hospital a few weeks before Christmas with 'farmer's lung' which is a condition normally caused by breathing in dust and chemical's associated with farming. Dad was really ill. The worst that I had ever seen him. My mum was worried sick about him and she was thin and losing weight and my sister had a new born baby and she was stressed out too. Dad was on a lot of medication, he had nebulisers and various drugs to clear his lungs, and he remained in hospital for quite a while. He was on a ward with lots of older men, and he was always talking to them about Jesus, even though he was really ill and feeling rotten. Guess you can't stop pastoring even when you're ill.

Jon and I went Christmas shopping in Exeter and we called in to visit Dad in the hospital on our way home, expecting him to be sitting up in bed, giving the rest of the ward a sermon, but instead we arrived only to find his bed empty. The other men in the ward were looking a bit concerned and they told us to find the ward sister and speak to her. She informed us that my Dad had taken a turn for the worse and had been admitted to intensive care. We rushed down the stairs and headed straight for the intensive care unit and when we arrived, we found my dad hooked up to lots of bleeping machinery, and my mother was holding vigil by his bedside. He looked like he was dying and he was only forty four at the time. He was unconscious and he had tubes attached to his chest and up his nose. I was terrified that I was about to lose my dad.

We stayed for a while, keeping mum company. My sister was pushing Laura up and down the corridor in a pram and trying to stay calm, but she was so stressed out that Laura was upset too, so eventually she went home, and Jon and I went back to the farm in Hemyock and to the boys we were fostering. We knew that later that evening, my Dad's church were holding a prayer meeting, especially for him, so I decided to go along and pray for my Dad with everyone else. I remember washing my hair and changing my clothes in a bit of a daze that evening, because up until now, my Dad had always been a very strong and capable man and I had never seen him look so helpless and vulnerable before. Just before Jon and I left for the prayer meeting, I got alone with God and I made a deal with him. I told him that if he would restore my Dad to full health and save his life, I would never ask for a baby again. I'd not have any children, I would just work full time for him, and I genuinely meant it. I didn't even feel sad about what I was giving up for my Dad, I just wanted my Dad back and I was willing to pay whatever it cost.

My Dad survived. He has a great testimony of what happened to him, and it was a very significant point in his life. Maybe he'll write a book and tell everyone all about it, but it's his story to tell, so I'll let him do it.

A few months later, we contacted Glyn and Shirley, told them enough was enough and we couldn't foster the boys anymore. They moved back into their house after having a break of ten months, and we moved back to our tiny little terrace house in Seaton, with our cat, our dog and another puppy that we had foolishly adopted, called Shaggy. Our house was full of hairy pets that made Jon sneeze, neither of us had a job, and there was no baby. Things weren't looking good, but I had stopped praying for a baby so I wasn't expecting life to get any better.

To really rub a huge dose of salt into our gaping wounds, our friends were popping babies out all over the place. One, by one, they would turn up to our home, nervous, and worried about how we would react when they told us their good news, because by now, all our friends knew that we were trying for a baby, and some of them had already guessed that we were having problems. I remember one of our friends standing in the kitchen of our home, after just telling us that they were expecting their first child, and he said that he thought we would have been the first to have a child. "I thought you'd be popping one out year after year for the next decade," he'd said. "Guess I was wrong."

I could have slapped him and trampled him into the carpet that night. What a stupid, insensitive thing to say. My chest was so tight from holding in the enormous wail of agony that was trying to burst out, that I could hardly breathe, and our insensitive friend didn't even notice. He prattled on about baby names, drank my coffee and left about an hour later. I was glad to see the back of him. I couldn't even speak to Jon, I just went to bed. My stomach was twisted tight, and I hated my friends for being pregnant. I wanted to punch the ceiling in my bedroom and open up a big hole so that I could scream at God at the injustice of it. They'd got pregnant in the first month of trying and no one knew or understood how we felt.

The final straw came when Jon's brother and his wife came to tell us that they were expecting their first child. I was in the bath at the time, and as soon as they arrived, I knew what was coming. I can remember sitting in the bath, hugging my knees to my chest and listening to Jon coming up the stairs. He knocked on the bathroom door and came in and sat on the loo and just looked at me.

"Are you coming down? They want to tell us their news."

"No," I shook my head. "Just tell them that I am really pleased for them, but that I'm not feeling great."

Jon just nodded, and went to face his brother alone. A few minutes later, I heard the front door open and close and I knew they had gone. I wanted to be happy for them, but that night I just couldn't fake it. I wasn't being a bitch, I was in pain. I'd had enough.

So my sister had a little girl, and my sister in law also gave birth to a little girl in 1993 called Bethany and they were the first grandchildren to be born on both sides of the family and I was screwed up with pain because I had so wanted to give my parents and parents in law their first grandchild. I'd done everything right, but had failed everyone. Michaela had a daughter too, Penny had a son and a daughter, Jane had a daughter and I had no one, just my wonderful Jon and three pets.

Was I happy that I had made a deal with God? Of course not. Had I told anyone what I had done? Nope, because they would have been upset and cross with me. Especially my Dad.

I had run out of options. I was sad to the point of depression. Jon was worried about me and disappointed that he wasn't going to be a dad any time soon and I couldn't do anymore. We'd done everything. We'd had sex at the right time and I'd even done handstands to make sure the sperm headed in the right direction afterwards. We'd given up caffeine and alcohol, and we were taking multivitamins every day. Jon wore baggy boxers and he took cold showers to keep everything cool and functioning properly. It didn't make any difference.

One evening, Jon decided to go to a church meeting in South Chard, with several other people from our church in Seaton. I only went because I had nothing better to do and I quite liked their funky style of worship. There was a guest speaker that night and I couldn't tell you what he preached. It was just a standard evening meeting, but that night God had something to say to me and Jon. At the end of the meeting, the preacher, Don Smythe, who had travelled all the way from Hong Kong to speak, walked down the centre of the church and looked directly at Jon.

"May I pray for you, sir?" he said, and Jon smiled and nodded. "Is this your wife?" he asked, looking at me.

"Yes," Jon replied.

"Would you come to the front please?"

We both stood up and walked to the front of the church in front of everyone, including a lot of people who had travelled from our church to hear the visiting speaker. He looked directly at us and said, "You don't have any children, do you?"

Jon held my hand. "No," he replied.

"Can I pray for you to have children?" he asked and Jon laughed.

"Yes, please," he said.

Don Smythe prayed a simple prayer over us that night, and once he had finished, we sat down with the rest of the congregation once more and that was it.

Within two weeks, I was pregnant with our first child. God had intervened and heard Don's prayer of faith, because Jon and I were worn out.

Harry was born June 1994 weighing exactly seven pounds. He took thirty nine hours to be delivered and he came out wailing, and did a wee all over the nurse. He was God's perfect blessing and proof that God was right about me. I was childless, not infertile as the doctors had said and Harry was born in God's perfect timing, not mine or Jon's. It took me years to understand that. Six long years to be precise. Harry is now eighteen and has just joined the Fire Service. He has a faith in God, which is awesome and God has plans for his life which are all in his perfect timing too.

Seth or Tamar

Harry was about eighteen months old, when we took him with us to a leader's conference in Swanwick. We were the only people there with a baby, but Harry was easy-going (he still is) and he slept a lot, so I was able to sit in the meetings along with everyone else and enjoy the seminars too.

We had our afternoon's free and we would spend time walking around the extensive grounds of the conference venue, pushing Harry around in his buggy and hoping he would have an afternoon nap so that we could talk. There was another couple staying at the venue, who had flown over from America for the conference and they were about our age, so we spent some time with them. Eric was born in America, but Sarah was Korean and adopted as a child by an American family. She explained to me that her American sister had recently adopted a little girl from China and I was very interested, because Jon and I had considered adoption as an option before Harry came along. Even though Harry was only a toddler, I was a little concerned that I hadn't conceived again since his birth because we hadn't been using any contraception, and yet eighteen months on and no sign of baby number two. The doctor had almost assured me that now we had managed to have Harry, my body would likely be kick-started into producing babies easily now. I'm not sure if that was just him trying to stop me from panicking again or whether there was any medical facts to go along with that statement, but the fact was that we were not expecting another child and we both wanted Harry to have a sibling.

Jon, initially wasn't keen about adopting from China. It wasn't the normal way that a white British couple added to their family and he felt that if we did go down the adoption route then why not adopt in the UK. He thought that it would be better to sponsor a Chinese child and help to pay for their education and health care, etc., rather than removing them from their home and dragging them halfway around the world.

I didn't agree.

I spoke to Sarah and asked her what she thought about child sponsorship and her answer was enough to convince Jon that perhaps we could look into the possibility of adopting from China. She told us that if she hadn't been adopted by her family, then she would have died. She felt she needed more than just money being sent to her, she needed a mum that would cuddle her and stop her from being afraid of the dark, and a dad who would protect her, and tell her about Jesus. I was practically jumping in the air in desperation when I heard that. All I wanted to do was cuddle and love a Chinese child that needed a mummy. I could do that. I knew it in my heart and poor Jon agreed that when we got home, we could make some enquiries about adopting from China.

It was almost as soon as we were in the door, that I was on the phone. I called social services and asked them all sorts of questions about adopting from China, and because it was a relatively new thing to do, they promised to look into it further and get back to me with the name of a social worker that would come and start a home study. Jon started looking into the finances and realised that there was no way we could afford to adopt from China. We were living on a really tight budget anyway, and the costs that he worked out, came to about £8,000.

We had just moved into a larger three bedroomed semi only a few months previously and the place was in dire need of work. We had no heating in the house at all, except for an open fire in the front room, the double glazing was so old that every time it rained, the water came in and filled up in between the two panes of glass and the bathroom had an old wrought iron bath with ball and claw feet, and it was originally put in, in 1936. It chugged out brown rusty water and everything smelled of mould. We had no money for any of the work and we were now talking about adopting a child, and one that was going to cost a small fortune.

So we prayed.

At this point in the story, I'm just going to tell you another story about me when I was a little girl because it'll help explain why this adoption was so important.

I've already told you that I grew up on a farm with my parents and my sister. Well, during the long summer holidays, my sister and I would plan what we were going to do to fill our time. In our bedroom which we shared, we had a huge cupboard that ran the length of the room and we used to make it into all sorts of things, our favourite being a dolly's hospital. We collected lots of cardboard boxes from the supermarket and made hospital beds for all our dolls and turned the cupboard into a hospital ward, I was matron, my sister was the cook and she made lots of dinners for the patients out of pastercine, rolling up vast numbers of brown sausages and green peas to make our dolls better.

One year, our cupboard got changed into an orphanage. It was about this time, that I moved out of our joint bedroom and got a bedroom of my own. I would spend hours and hours making rag dolls in my room. They came in every colour you could imagine and they were made out of my nana's curtain lining, and stuffed with my parents underwear. My poor dad lost all his socks, one year and I'm still not sure if he knows what happened to them even to this day. My sister would stand outside my bedroom door and ask me if the baby had arrived yet, meaning, have you sewn the dolly yet. I'd be madly sewing, telling her that the orphanage had phoned and it was arriving very soon. I must have made twenty multicultural dolls that year, and every one of them had a name appropriate to the country that it came from, and I adopted them all.

I was about ten when I was shopping in our local town with my mum, and I saw a Chinese woman carrying a Chinese baby over her shoulder. We didn't have a lot of Chinese people in our Devon town at that time, so it was an unusual sight, that's why I clearly remember what I said to my mother at the time. I told my mother that when I was older, I was going to have a Chinese baby and she reminded me of that when I told her that Jon and I were going to adopt a Chinese child. At the time my mother just smiled and told me that I would have to marry a Chinese man, but I truly believe that God planted that seed of adopting from China in my heart when I was young and tender and not so full of disbelief, and that over time, that seed began to flourish in my heart as a real possibility.

So back to the story. Jon and I were skint, and our families thought that we ought to get our house sorted out as a priority and be grateful for having Harry, which of course we were, but we knew that adopting from China was right for us, so we pressed forward, praying that God would somehow do a miracle and pay the £8,000 that we needed to proceed. Today the total cost is closer to £20,000.

Social Services were going to charge us £500, to be assessed as perspective overseas adopters. (Today 2012 it's at least £3,000) They didn't charge anything to adopt a British child, but we pressed on regardless because we knew this was right for us. We also knew that our costs would soon start mounting up and we still didn't have any money. It was a huge step of faith and one we would not have undertaken had we not had a green light from God. It came in the post one morning, completely out of the blue, and I was so excited, I remember dancing around the kitchen.

A friend whom I had not seen for several years after she had disappeared off to university, sent me a cheque for £80 and a short note which said;

Hi Louise, I know this is a bit odd, but God told me you needed this, so it's yours. What are you up to?

Love Kate. xx

Kate had sent us exactly enough money to pay for our medicals that social services wanted us to have. Normally they would have paid for the medicals, but again, because the child we wanted wasn't British, we had to pay for everything ourselves. Jon and I knew that God had everything under control. We didn't have £8,000 in our bank account because we didn't need all of it yet, but bit by bit, the money came. People heard what we were doing and gave us money. Other people held car boot sales and jumble sales for us and when it came to pay social services for the assessment, the fee was only £350 instead of

£500 and we had exactly enough money to pay for that, with no effort on our part.

The assessment took eighteen months and on the day that we found out that we had been approved to adopt from China, we had a serious car accident.

We were coming home from Christmas shopping and Harry was in a car seat in the back, when we were hit by a car that was trying to avoid another car at a junction. Our airbags failed to deploy and to this day, I can still remember hearing Harry screaming in the seat behind me. Our car was completely destroyed and the only portion of the car to be completely undamaged was my seat, Jon's seat and Harry's seat, the rest of the car was buckled into a twisted wreck. We had bought Harry a painting easel for Christmas, and 'miraculously' it had slid up into the air, right behind Harry's seat and prevented all of us from being pelted on the backs of our heads with giant cans of dog food that we had also purchased that day. The painting easel had saved our lives, and taken the full impact of our shopping, rather than our heads. The car accident should have killed us all, but God was in control that day. Someone else was not happy that we were adopting from China.

In June the following year, a day before Harry's third birthday, I wasn't feeling particularly well. The previous weekend I had catered a dinner party for friends and shopping for the food had been extremely difficult. I had shooting pains in the front of my thighs, and cramping pains in my vagina which I thought was all to do with my period. By the Monday morning, after spending most of Sunday in bed feeling flu like, I could barely walk. I strapped Harry into his high chair to have his breakfast, and kissed Jon goodbye as he headed off to work. When I reached the kitchen, I suddenly felt as if I couldn't stand up and my legs buckled underneath me.

Suddenly Jon was with me because he had returned to the house, after forgetting his debit card to get some petrol. He phoned the doctors surgery and after dropping Harry over to my sister's house, he helped me walked into the clinic where I collapsed onto the long padded seats and curled up into a little ball. The doctor and Jon had to carry me into his room. He took one look at me, and sent me straight into hospital, with a suspected ectopic pregnancy. Jon and I talked as we travelled into hospital and we just couldn't believe that the doctor was right.

As soon as we arrived, we knew that whatever was wrong with me was serious because medical staff were waiting for me to arrive. I was helped onto a commode and told to pee, and my pee was full of blood. They shoved a large plastic tube into a vein in my arm so that they could get drugs into my system as quickly as possible, just in case I collapsed again and the pregnancy result came back positive. I was actually pregnant and they were preparing to remove it.

I cannot even begin to express how desperate and railroaded I felt at that moment. People were shouting at other members of staff to get me prepped for theatre and I had lost any say over my body. I was pregnant, actually pregnant and now they were going to take it away.

I still find this difficult to talk about. Writing this now, my chest is tight and my eyes are full of tears. I'm trying to be brave, but I'm still grieving this loss.

I'd heard somewhere that an ectopic pregnancy had survived and one woman had grown a baby on the outside of her uterus, so I tried to tell the doctor that I wanted to do the same, but he wasn't listening. I tried to tell him that I was a Christian and I didn't believe in abortion, but he was too busy trying to book me into emergency surgery and he still wasn't listening. Then I remembered a woman who had also had an ectopic pregnancy, but she had been expecting twins and one of the babies was in her womb and was viable, so I demanded that the doctor check where the pregnancy was and he looked at me like I was nuts, but agreed to give me an internal scan.

The internal scan hurt me so much, that I was almost lifting off the bed in agony. He looked in all the right places, and I was willing him to find a baby's heartbeat in my womb, but it was not there.

"Look, if I just wait and see what happens, just in case it's too small for you to find, what would happen?" I asked him in desperation.

"If I don't go ahead and do the procedure, you'll be dead in an hour," he said. "And you've got a son to think about who needs his mum."

I gritted my teeth, asked God to forgive me for what I was about to do, and I signed the paperwork. They rushed me into the operating theatre and a nurse held my hand and smiled at me.

"I want this baby," I sobbed, hoping for a last minute reprieve.

"I know, dear, but this is not a viable pregnancy, and we're saving your life," she said. Then I went to sleep.

I woke up and was informed that they had removed a sizable obstruction to my Fallopian tube, (I presume they meant my child) and they had also removed my Fallopian tube which was badly scarred due to an appendix operation that I'd had when I was eighteen. One of the doctors had referred to it as an abortion and I was disgusted with his comment. I was heartbroken, I still am, but to him, I was just another patient whom he had already forgotten.

It was Harry's third birthday the following day and I sat up in bed trying to look excited and happy for him as he opened his presents on my hospital bed. My parents in law brought him into hospital and told him that I had a bad tummy and the doctors were making me better. We sang happy birthday and he blew out the candles on his cake and looked happy, and my sister took him out for the day with her little boy, so he didn't miss out on celebrating, but it is a part of my life that I have never forgotten, and I bear the scars that remind me that I was pregnant, but didn't have the baby.

Jon and I were told that the chances of us ever having another child were nil, so we accepted the doctor's opinion, and set our hearts on adopting from China. Everything was still proceeding and we were just waiting to hear from the Chinese authorities. Jon and I would have a little boy and a little girl and our family would be complete.

So why Seth or Tamar? Because that's what I would have named the baby, if he or she had been born. I don't know if he or she is a girl or a boy, but I want them to have a name in heaven with Jesus. I am confident that I will meet them one day and that's why he or she *is* called Tamar or Seth, not *was* called. Their soul is not lost and I believe that I will still have a relationship with them in eternity one day.

Le Chang

In September 1998 the Yangtze river flooded and many people lost their lives. We weren't expecting to adopt from China until early 1999, but we suddenly received a letter from China, with details of a baby girl called Le Chang, who was six months old. The Welfare Institute that she was living in, had been severely damaged by flooding and they were rehoming the orphans as quickly as possible. I was so excited that I could hardly contain myself.

We'd received a medical with her paperwork, but it was all written in Chinese, which makes sense to them but not to us. So we headed off to our local Chinese takeaway and asked them if they could translate it for us. We'd never met them before, other than to buy Kung Po Chicken and Sweet and Sour Pork, but they were so lovely and welcoming and they invited us into their home. They were able to translate everything for us except for a small amount of medical information. Most of us would find British medical's hard to comprehend, so they suggested we went and spoke to a Chinese doctor or a herbalist. The local hospital didn't have any Chinese doctors currently employed with them, and I ended up phoning a Chinese alternative healing place in Exeter and asking them if they could help. They agreed to look at the medical, but they were going to charge me £5.00 a sentence!

At the time I didn't drive a car, so my father-in-law said that he would drive me into Exeter and I was determined to catch the evening post, so it was a bit of a mad dash. My mother-in-law came too, and we ran down the high street as quickly as possible before the shop closed. As soon as I got to the shop, I realised that I had no money, but my lovely mother-in-law said that she would pay for the translator so I looked at the Chinese man and I pointed at just one sentence, and asked him to translate it for me.

You see, the problem was that because Jon and I already had a child, Chinese policy said that we couldn't have a 'perfect child', we had to have a child that was not perfect, meaning that she had some kind of disability, so it was crucial that we knew exactly what was wrong with this little baby girl that we had been offered. I could see him scanning the whole document with his eyes and then he looked at me and smiled.

"She has soft, big head," he said.

Hydrocephalus?

"Bent limbs," he said.

Spina bifida?

"But her eyes are good," he said finally.

I took a deep breath, knowing that my mother-in-law was listening to everything that her potential granddaughter had too, and was probably worried sick.

"Her eyes are good?" I asked.

He nodded and smiled. "She's fine," he said and nodded.

She's fine? Was that code for something? Fine meant fine, right?

My mother-in-law paid the man, and we made another mad dash back up through the high street towards the post office. I pulled out my mobile phone and dialled Jon's number at work, then relayed everything that the Chinese herbalist had said. We knew that as soon as we signed the paperwork and sent it back to China, it was a legally binding contract to adopt Le Chang and there would be no going back.

I stood in the post office queue, and decided to sign the paperwork. We could have sent it back and asked for another child, but Jon and I both felt that we could not have lived with that decision. Imagine always wondering what happened to the child that you rejected? We weren't prepared to do that, but we were prepared to accept a severely disabled child and love her, no matter what.

We knew that there was another couple who lived near us in Exeter and they were waiting to hear about a child from China too, but when I spoke to them on the phone, they seemed to think that the arrangements to travel to China would take a little longer than I thought and that I was getting over excited prematurely.

I was sure that things were going to happen quickly. I could feel it in my gut. It was more than just gut instinct, it was God instinct, so Jon and I made enquiries about flights to China, and accommodation and tour guides, etc. and then God instinct was proved right, when within a week we had been sent an invitation to travel to China and to meet and collect our new daughter.

*****

At this point in the story, I think I'd better explain how big a wuss I am when it comes to flying. I hate it. It's doesn't come from an irrational fear, but one that is based on the fact that one holiday to the Canary Islands started with us making an emergency landing at Gatwick airport. There were ambulances, fire engines and police everywhere as we made our descent with no hydraulics, and consequently, no landing gear. The cabin crew was terrified, and gripping their seats with white knuckles, I was shaking with fear and convinced that we were about to die in a plane crash, and Jon was praying. We survived, you probably already guessed that, but it was terrifying and from that moment onwards, I had a real problem flying in planes.

That's not so great when you know that in order to get your Chinese daughter, you have to take six flights before you are back home again. Our first flight was from Bristol to Amsterdam, and I started to panic the moment we got on the plane. Jon grabbed hold of my arm and told me to sit down and shut up, but instead, I unbuckled my seat and ran down the centre aisle of the plane in a panic. I stood by the door that hadn't closed on us yet and the air stewardess looked worried and asked me if I was ok. These days, with the extra security on planes, I would have been knocked out and arrested for being a menace, but instead, the lovely girl offered me Valium and a large brandy! I declined both, and pulled myself together, managing to get back in my seat with only a few people giving me weird looks, and about ten minutes into the journey, the air steward turned up at my seat and asked me if I would like to have a seat with the captain! How cool was that? I left Jon behind and spent the rest of the flight sitting in the cockpit with the captain and his second in command, eating sandwiches and drinking orange juice and looking out of the huge windows as we came into land at Schiphol airport.

I'd calmed down a bit by the time we took our main flight to Beijing. Jon thought that it was funny that I was acting like a moron in front of everyone, but I didn't care. It was a very memorable trip to Amsterdam and one that sadly would never happen again because of all the increased security that has now become part of our everyday life.

Once we had arrived in Beijing, we had a very long wait at the airport to catch an internal flight. Jon and I sat next to a crowd of Chinese travellers who smiled politely at us and were playing small board games to wile away the time. I had a large tube of Pringles, which I'd bought from home, so I shared them around and they accepted crisps from me, but you could tell they thought I was a bit odd. A big, blonde, white, weird woman with a tube of sour cream Pringles in the middle of Beijing airport. Nothing odd about that at all.

Our internal flight was worrying. We were both a little concerned that the plane looked 'old', and even more concerned when all of the Chinese passengers refused the food on board. We ate it, and discovered why no one else was eating it. We bumped and jolted our way across China, along with a hundred other people and I had never prayed so hard for God's protection, as I did on that flight.

It had been an extremely long day, and after hours and hours of travelling, we finally arrived in Nanchang in the early evening, knowing that in the following morning, we would finally get to meet the little girl that was destined to be our daughter.

As soon as we had arrived at the small internal airport, we were treated like royalty. Our luggage was collected for us and we were appointed a guide who saw to everything for us. We climbed aboard a minibus that was waiting for us just outside the airport terminal and pretty much 'took off', as we sped through the streets of downtown Nanchang. We swerved to avoid an accident that had happened shortly before, and I was shocked to see dead bodies on the road, that were covered with sheets. It had been raining and the street lights and the greasy windows, fuzzed everything so it was difficult to see what the rest of the scenery was like around us. The city was bustling, noisy and crowded with lots of people on bikes and various other modes of transport, whizzing past our windows and hurtling off to their numerous destinations.

We were shortly deposited outside our hotel and as soon as we stepped outside of the minibus, the smell hit us. The air was warm, you could smell the rain and the hot, tarmac road and there was a taste of fuel and food cooking, in the air too. It was completely unique and I was nervously excited about what we were about to do.

As soon as we stepped into the hotel foyer, it was like walking into a completely different world. There was a fountain spouting water into the air, right in front of the reception desk and the floors were polished marble. There were giant ceiling fans and dangling crystal lights above our heads and people were bowing at us.

The guide led us up to our room and two maids came in, asked us to sit on the chairs and they removed our shoes and put slippers on our feet, then they made us tea and turned down the beds for us. We noticed that there was a cot in our bedroom, with very lovely baby bedding in it and the Chinese people were treating us like we were very important people.

We were left alone and I was still reeling from the fact that we were actually in China. We'd come such a long way, with absolutely no money, and no experience, just trusting that God knew what he was doing and everything was going to work out ok.

Then our phone rang, and it was the receptionist from the front desk informing us that our baby had arrived and she was coming up in the lift, with her child minder.

I was speechless. We weren't expecting to meet her until the following morning. Jon was in the loo, so I hammered on the bathroom door and told him to hurry up because our daughter was arriving and then I opened the bedroom door and watched as a Chinese woman carrying a baby, and accompanied by two very large Chinese male bouncers, stepped out of the hotel lift and walked towards me.

I nervously stood next to Jon, and watched as a tiny bundle was placed on one of our beds and the Chinese woman who had been carrying the baby stepped back and looked at me.

I didn't know what to do. I just stared at the baby lying motionless on the bed and it wasn't until Jon nudged me, that I snapped out of it, leaned down and picked Lily up.

As soon as I held her, I loved her. I absolutely adored her straight away. She had almost opaque black eyes and she was so tiny that I knew all of the clothes that we had brought with us were going to swamp her. The Chinese woman informed us that she would meet us in the morning to sign all the legal paperwork and we were left with this strange new baby, who didn't make a sound.

As soon as the door closed, it was action stations. We had excellent facilities in our room for heating and making a bottle of milk. We'd bought milk formula, bottles, teats and sterilisation kit with us. She took a full 8oz bottle straight off and then she burped loudly, but she looked completely emotionless and vacant. The next thing I did was strip her and give her a bath. She was wearing a long sleeved top and trousers with the gusset cut out around her bottom and she was wrapped in a towel. Her head had been shaved, and she had a little tuft of hair at the front where they had missed a bit. She had two front teeth and a tiny little nose and she was absolutely adorable. As far as I could see there was nothing wrong with her head. The soft spot was still soft because she was much younger than the medical had said she was, so that was perfectly normal, and she didn't have Hydrocephalus, however she was in a very poor state of health. All along her jaw, and her collar bone there was a wide band of purple bruising with lumps that you could wobble with your fingertips, and my biggest fear was that she had skin cancer. She was a pitiful sight, but I absolutely loved her. I bathed her gently, and I put nappy cream on her sore bottom, dressed her in her new soft clothes and put some baby cream on the skin on her sore neck, and she relaxed and went straight to sleep, lying on my bed, as I stroked her throat.

I sat up all night watching her. I couldn't believe that this was her. When she woke for a bottle, she just lay there in the cot and didn't make a sound. She didn't cry. She didn't gurgle or coo, she was silent. She was used to no attention, so she didn't ask for it and it broke my heart.

I sat on the bed, cuddling her, kissing her and talking to her, telling her that I loved her and she was going to have a good life. She had no idea what I was saying and she was probably terrified of me, but she had been given into our safe keeping by God for a purpose, and we were up for the challenge.

The following day, we headed off downstairs, exhausted through lack of sleep, nervous about what the day would bring, and worried about all the technicalities of adopting a child from China, and we met a whole bunch of American's who were also staying in the hotel, and had also received their daughters last night, just like us. They were also tired like us and had been up all night, watching over their precious little girls too.

We spent the morning doing all the legal aspect of the adoption. We had to promise in front of a Chinese judge that we would love and care for our daughter and that we would never abandon her, which of course, we did. We were given a white china elephant in a blue silk box as a gift, and then we were bundled back into the large minibus with the rest of the American adopters and we all headed out for the day to visit a beautiful Chinese palace. It was surreal. This was the culmination of months of planning, fund raising and praying, and now we were finally here in China with our new daughter, Lily Grace Le Chang, walking around a Chinese palace, with a bunch of American's that we had never met before, as if it was a perfectly normal thing to do.

That evening, I voiced my concerns about Lily's neck and throat, to one of the single adoptive mothers that was part of the American party, and to my surprise and delight, she turned out to be a paediatrician. She told me to come up to her hotel room after dinner and she would take a look at Lily's neck.

The doctor was a blessing straight from God. She gave Lily a full medical, allayed all my fears about hydrocephalus and spina bifida, putting her twisted arms and legs down to being swaddled tightly as a newborn and not given any exercise. She opened up her sizable suitcase which turned out to be a portable pharmacy, and she gave me, free of charge, anti-bacterial cream for Lily's skin, and antibiotics for any infection that she had in her ears.

On day three of our stay in China, we had the joy of seeing Lily smile for the first time in her life. Jon was sitting on the bed bouncing her on his knee and clapping her hands together and suddenly she giggled. I was in the bathroom getting ready to go down for breakfast, and Jon told me to come and watch. He clapped her hands together again and she giggled again and it felt like we had finally had a breakthrough. She had suddenly come back to life, and we were absolutely thrilled.

We had one major hurdle to overcome whilst we were out in China and that was our travel arrangements. We needed to fly back to Beijing to get a visa and a passport for Lily to travel to the UK and then we had to fly home on tickets that were not changeable. When we had booked our flights, we had got a special deal because the tickets had fixed dates for travelling. It meant that if we didn't catch our flight home, we would have to buy new tickets for all three of us, at a cost of a couple of thousand pounds. We've already said that money was tight, and the whole trip was budgeted down to the last penny, so buying new tickets was not an option. But in order for Lily to fly on the plane to Beijing, she had to have some extra paperwork that we needed for her visa, and we were informed at breakfast by the guide that the office was closed and we weren't going to have the paperwork in time to catch the flight.

It was a huge disaster. We had to be on that flight, but the guide insisted that the office was closed on a Tuesday and that was it.

So we prayed.

We also phoned my parents and asked them to pray too, and by breakfast the following day, the guide came to tell us that the people who worked in the office were going to open up especially for us, and that the paperwork would be ready for us to fly back to Beijing. He also added that it was unprecedented and he couldn't believe what had happened.

Jon and I had a huge smirk on our faces because we knew exactly what had happened and who was in control.

We flew home with Lily in November 1998 and arrived at Bristol airport on the last of our six flights, exhausted, excited, and the proud parents of two miracle children. All our family were there to greet us, and Harry met his sister for the first time. His thoughts on meeting his sister? He thought she was "wiggly and smelled funny".

*****

There are a lot of children in the world that need sponsoring. Not everyone wants to, or can adopt from overseas, but many more people could sponsor a child in their own country, and help pay towards their food, clothing and education. Please prayerfully consider this. There are a number of organisations who you could contact and they are easy to find on the internet. For most children who are sponsored, it is the difference between existing, and actually living.

Jesse

When I had suffered the ectopic pregnancy, I had foolishly worked out that the baby I was carrying, would have been born on Valentines Day in 1999. As the weeks ticked on past Christmas and into the New Year, I subconsciously worked out how pregnant I would have been by now, had everything gone to plan.

I didn't know why I was torturing myself, by constantly reminding myself of the baby that died, but I did, and even though I was happy, and content with my two amazing children, my heart was still grieving over the loss of my baby. I had a scar on my arm where they had put the thick, plastic tube into my arm and every time I saw the scar, it reminded me of that day when I had lost control, and fear and pain had taken over. I still look at the scar even now and remember how close I came to dying. If Jon hadn't come home for his debit card, Harry would have been strapped in his high chair all day, and I would have been dead in the kitchen. God saved my life, of that I am very sure.

We had a fantastic first Christmas with Lily and we were interviewed for the local press and we were on the TV too. It was all very embarrassing, but they were looking for a heart warming story for Christmas and we were it. Lily had been in hospital with pneumonia and she was out just in time for Christmas, so everyone wanted to know her story.

We settled into family life and I decided that I wanted to try for another baby, so Jon and I talked about it and we decided to go for it. The doctors had told us that it wasn't going to happen, and now that I only had one Fallopian tube, things were looking pretty bleak, but we decided to try anyway, and with Valentine's day coming up, I planned a nice romantic evening, and thought that it would be the perfect opportunity to try for a baby.

But just a few days before Valentine's day in 1999, the day that the other baby should have been born, my period was already late, and with butterflies the size of baby elephants charging around my stomach, I secretly did a pregnancy test, and to my absolute delight I was already pregnant. I phoned Jon at work and told him over the phone because I couldn't wait for him to get home, and then I made an appointment to see my lovely, but slightly sceptical doctor.

"I'm pregnant," I said and grinned at him.

"Are you sure?" he frowned.

"YEP!" I smiled. "But I want a scan to make sure that it's in the right place."

He arranged it immediately and I headed off to the hospital to get one of the earliest scans possible. I had to drink so much fluid to get the best chance of a picture that I could barely walk. I was convinced that I was going to wet myself, but as I lay on the bed, and she moved the scanner over my lower stomach, she confirmed that there was a pregnancy and it was in my womb.

Then she went and told me how many pregnancies ended in miscarriage and how early everything was and I shouldn't get my hopes up. I nodded politely, got in the car and then I *loudly*, flatly refused to accept a single word that well-meaning but faithless nurse had said to me. I prayed over my baby every night, and every week that I was pregnant, I thanked God for blessing me again. I got bigger and more pregnant and then on November 17th, 1999, our second son, Jesse came wailing into the world, weighing 8lbs and miracle baby number three had joined our family.

In the space of a year, we had gained two more children and our lives were completely chaotic. We had two dogs, three children, no money, and Jon kept being made redundant. Our house still had no heating, and the old double glazing windows were half-full with water. All our furniture was second hand and shabby-chic was much too good to describe our home. I made the curtains and did most of the decorating with any leftover paint that my Uncle Brian, who was a painter and decorator, gave me. Our house was eclectic, full of toys, kids and dogs and we loved it and were blessed beyond words.

Thomas

So we decided that to round off the family nicely, we would adopt another girl. Two boys and two girls and that would be perfect. Well, that's what we thought anyway, but God was in control and he had another plan.

After Jesse was born another pregnancy didn't happen naturally and so we decided to look at adoption again, hoping that perhaps we could go back to China and adopt another little girl that would not only look more like Lily, but would also have a similar background and we would perhaps be able to help another little girl that so desperately needed parents. But when we looked into the adoption process, a lot of things had changed, and we no longer fulfilled the criteria for Chinese adoption. Our salary was so poor that we only earned half of what the Chinese government wanted us to earn, so our plans for adopting from China again, were put on hold.

We had always wanted to adopt from the UK, and many years ago it had been our first choice, so we phoned up our local social services office and a couple of weeks later, Brenda Thomas arrived at our house to begin the lengthy approval process all over again. Everything was different this time because we already had three children and we had fostered children too, before we had Harry, and we were considered a mixed race family because Lily was now part of us too, so we hoped that we would be considered for children of a different race too. By the time we were approved to adopt a child from the UK, Jesse was already three, Lily was four and about to start primary school, and Harry was eight. A lot of people thought that adopting another child was going to be a bit of a handful, but Jon and I were sure that it was the right thing to do. The adoption panel met to decide whether we were suitable or not, and thankfully we were approved to adopt one child between the ages of 0 and 3. We were over the moon and expecting it to happen instantly. We knew that there were hundreds of children waiting for their 'forever family', and we eagerly looked through 'Be my parent' magazines at all the cute faces of children that were needing homes, but every child that we phoned up about, was apparently not suitable for us.

Having Lily in our family made no difference at all. We were white, middle class, living in Devon, which was predominantly white, and social workers weren't interested in us at all. Every month the 'Be my parent' magazine would drop through our door, and our social worker, Brenda and I, would go through all the children and work out which ones would be suitable for our family. Then we would split the list between us and phone every social worker we could until we got the chance to speak to them and try and sell ourselves as perspective adopters. We even had A5 flyers printed up about us and our children, and we sent them to every social services office we possibly could in the hope that they would like the look of us and place a child with us. We made enquiries about eighty different children from every ethnic background, but no one was interested in us at all. It was demoralising and a lot of people would have given up and thought, 'well, we've got three children already, we might as well forget it,' but we didn't.

We were finally phoned by a social worker in Wales who had seen our flyer and wanted to meet us. He told us that he had a little girl who might be suitable and arrangements were made for us to travel to Cardiff with Brenda our social worker, to meet with the social worker and the child's foster mother. I was very excited. The little girl was two, and she had been fostered from birth, so she had good attachments to her foster mother. Some of you might think that's not so great because she was already bonded with another mother figure, but actually it meant that she would find it easier to bond with a new mother figure too, so I was feeling very positive about this. That was until we met the foster mother.

We sat in a dark, old office with the social worker, the foster mother and our social worker and I knew the whole thing was wrong. I felt it in my gut. It might have been God instinct, or gut instinct, I'm not completely sure, but either way, I didn't feel right. What the child's social worker had failed to tell us was that the little girl had Foetal Alcohol Syndrome (FAS), and she had severe learning disabilities. The foster mother told us everything and the social worker looked really embarrassed that he had been caught lying to us. It wasn't the fact that the little girl had health problems, because at the beginning, Lily had potentially very serious problems, it was the fact that the social worker had blatantly lied to us, and we were both really cross about the whole situation.

FAS was something that we didn't feel we would be able to cope with and I was confident that we wouldn't receive any help from her social worker if we needed it, because I didn't trust him.

The child had other complicated medical needs and the social worker thought that by showing us how cute and pretty she was, that we'd be begging to adopt her, but we had both said before the trip that if one of us didn't feel happy or relaxed about anything, then we wouldn't go ahead with it. Unfortunately, neither of us felt happy, and we decided to leave and go home. Our social worker was furious on our behalf that we had been tricked into coming all the way to Wales, and she wrote a letter saying so.

But we believed that God had called us to do this, and so we persevered, and then finally the 'Be my Parent' magazine dropped through our letter-box, and inside was a tiny little picture of a little baby boy that needed a Christian family.

His write up was not good and there were a lot of health concerns, but the fact that they were looking for a Christian family for him, meant that we possibly had a chance. I phoned up Brenda and she'd already spotted the child and was going to phone me, so I contacted the child's social worker and to my annoyance she wasn't in. That meant waiting for her to contact me. I paced the kitchen that day, willing the phone to ring and eventually it did and I spoke to a woman called Sharon who was finally interested in our family.

Arrangements were made for Sharon and another social worker to visit us and Brenda was with us too. As soon as we saw a picture of the little boy for the first time, I just knew he was the one for us. Lots of people say that, when they first see a picture of the child that they want to adopt, but I knew it in my gut. I felt like God was saying, 'yes'. But it wasn't up to us. The social workers had to decide. They waited for Harry to come home from school because they wanted to ask him how he felt about sharing his mummy and daddy with another child when he already had to share them with Lily and Jesse, and I wasn't sure what kind of a mood Harry was going to be in when he was tired and hungry and just back from school, but Harry was a star.

He came in and sat on the sofa and the first thing he did was hug Jesse. Jesse was shy and nervous of the social workers and so Harry put his arm around him as if it was the most natural thing in the world and he talked to the social workers perfectly, telling them that he would like another brother, because he didn't like girls, except his sister.

Believe it or not, it swung it. They loved the way that Harry loved his brother and was protective of him, and they felt that he would make a brilliant older brother for this little boy.

A few weeks later we were invited to the adoption panel in Westminster and we were very nervous. There were about twenty people sitting around a table, with all our private, personal details right in front of them in black and white, and they were going to ask us questions about why we wanted to adopt this specific child.

It was the single, most intimidating moment that I can recall. They were all from London, and we were the visiting country bumpkins. I felt as if I wasn't dressed right, and I should have worn my mother's trouser suit. The lack of finances came up, which wasn't a surprise, and the fact that the child was not white and English, was also raised, but thankfully Tom's social worker was Jamaican and she spoke up for us. She told them that regardless of the colour of our skin, we were the best people to parent Tom, and she liked us. She said that our family was wonderful, and that Tom would have a good life with us. I felt very emotional. Then she said that we were Christians, and that it was Tom's birth mother's wishes that he be brought up in a Christian family, so as far as she was concerned, there was no one better.

I imagined doing a silent 'high-five' with God, when she said that and I remembered a Bible verse, that was written on the front of a bible and given to Jon and I when we got married.

"If God is for us, then who can be against us," Romans 8 v31.

God was in control. Once the panel had made the recommendation that we would be suitable as Tom's parents, we headed back to the social services office to make plans for how we were going to meet Tom and eventually take over his parenting. We met with his foster mother, who had cared for Tom since he was a few days old, and understandably she was very upset that Tom was going to be leaving her care. Tom has been just one week away from his first birthday, so she had been the only mother figure that he had known. She was also a born again Christian, and along with her husband and church, had been praying that a Christian family would be found for Tom, but when we came along, it was not only a happy and exciting time for us, but it was an emotionally sad time for her and her family and something that we would all have to work through over the coming few days.

A schedule was worked out where we would spend a few days in London, getting to know Tom and every aspect of his care, and then at the end of the few days, the foster family would travel down to Devon, with all of Tom's belongings and his care would then be passed to me, but they would still be here for a couple of days just in case he was distressed and didn't settle.

I was nervous. I didn't know how I was going to get on with this other mother figure in Tom's life. I didn't know his little habits and she had been everything to him.

Our other children went to stay with my sister, and Jesse was very upset and didn't want his mummy and daddy to go. We phoned the children every day before school and every night at bedtime, but Jesse would cry every time and it was really upsetting.

The first time we met Tom was at the foster carer's house. We rang on the doorbell and the foster mum welcomed us into her home and Tom was busy crawling across the hall floor towards us. We were told to take things nice and slow and not to overwhelm him, but as soon as I saw his cute, little chubby cheeks and his mass of curly dark hair, I scooped him up from the floor and gave him a cuddle. At exactly the same time, I somehow managed to switch on my mobile phone in my jacket pocket and dialled my sister, so she heard every word that we said, the first time we met Tom. Even today, my sister still laughs when she says that she was shouting her head off at me, in my pocket and I never heard a thing because I was too busy going gooey over my new baby.

Tom was a very poorly baby from birth. He was allergic to paracetamol, and would be violently sick if he had any paracetamol medicine, but he regularly needed pain relief because he often got ear infections, and chest infections, so for poor Tom his first few months were nothing but hospital visits, and medication for various ailments.

We visited at breakfast time and gave him his breakfast, we changed his nappy, took him out in his buggy around the local park, and put him down for a nap. It definitely helped that we were already parents, otherwise doing all of that under the watchful eye of the foster parent would have been much more daunting. We also gave him his bedtime bath, read stories to him, and tucked him up in bed at night time. Every aspect of his life, we had to learn in a few days before he was handed over to us for good. Another aspect of his life were his grandparents. Social services wanted us to have face to face contact with his grandparents once a year, and I wasn't remotely happy about this. Tom's birth mother wasn't going to have any contact with him, but Tom's mother's parents wanted to see their one and only grandson, which was completely understandable, so we agreed to meet with them to decide whether we thought that any kind of contact arrangements could be made. They were separated and lived in different countries, so contact was going to be tricky.

We met Granddad first and he was a lovely old man who clearly loved his grandson very much. He had wanted to look after Tom himself, but he wasn't physically able to do so. The demands of a new baby, would have been much too much for him and he was struggling to not feel guilty about this. I liked Granddad a lot. He was a gentleman, and an academic. He was well spoken, gentle and patient and it wasn't his fault that his daughter couldn't care for her child. Jon and I didn't want Granddad to pay the price and lose out on a relationship with Tom, or indeed for Tom to miss out on a relationship with his real Granddad.

Then we met Grandma, and she wasn't anything like I was expecting. She was bright, interesting, intelligent and also clearly loved Tom. I expected to be intimidated by her, because I knew that she was sussing us out too, and she was worried about who was going to be caring for her grandson.

"I suppose you will change his name?" she asked.

"No, he's going to be Tom," I replied.

"But I won't be his grandmother anymore," she said. "Your parent's will be his grandparents."

"Yes, they will, but you will always be his grandmother too," I reassured her. "Tom can have three Grandmother's and three Grandfather's."

"Can I buy him clothes?" she asked.

I smiled. Thank you God! "Yes, please," I replied. "That would be great."

So Grandma and I struck up a deal that day. She would be his Grandmother, and I would be his mother. We would meet up with her, and Granddad once a year to have a meal together and for them to see Tom and play with him, and we would write to both of them twice a year and send photos, and she would reply and send photo's back to Tom.

In practise it actually works much better than that. Tom is now nine and we see his Grandparents faithfully every year around his birthday. They generously lavish him with gifts of clothing and toys, and they always give us huge amounts of posh chocolates and special biscuits for our other children, which is very generous of them. Grandma and I get on very well together and we are on first name terms. After having lunch with her and Granddad a few times, Jon and I decided to give Grandma our home telephone number so that she could phone Tom whenever she wanted to. She doesn't live near us, so regular visiting is not possible. Tom loves seeing his Grandparents, and he understands why he looks like he does and why he likes art and sport. He's artistic like his grandmother and he enjoys sports like his granddad. We could have selfishly refused contact with his birth family and kept Tom all to ourselves, but Tom's best interests have always come first and if in later life his grandparents were no longer here and he hadn't had the chance to meet them, then that would have been very hard on him, and we didn't want that.

So today in 2014, our miracle children are aged nineteen, fifteen, fourteen and ten. When we look back over their stories, we can see how God was in control of their arrival every time, even though it was always frustrating and hard to wait for them to arrive. When our children were younger and they didn't know how babies were made, they assumed that you either prayed for a baby or you adopted one. Either way, a sister was a sister and a brother was a brother, no matter how they arrived in their family.

Women in the bible who were just like us

It's amazing how many women in the bible had problems conceiving and having children. I think the most obvious woman that almost always springs to mind is Hannah, so I'm going to retell her story in my way. You can read it for yourself in 1Samuel chapter 1v 1, right through to chapter 2 v 21inclusive.

Hannah

Elkanah and his two wives lived in Ramah. His wives were called Peninnah and Hannah. Peninnah had children with Elkanah, but Hannah was childless and this caused a lot of problems within their family.

Every year, the whole family travelled to Shiloh because it was required of every Israelite male to make a sacrifice to God Almighty and thank him for the blessings of fruitfulness and harvest. It was especially difficult for Hannah because year after year, she was constantly reminded of the fact that she was not fruitful, and Peninnah would taunt Hannah and tease her about the fact that she had no children by their husband, when she did.

When the time came for the sacrifice, Elkanah would give his wife Peninnah and each of her children a portion of meat, and because he felt sorry for Hannah, he would give her a double portion of meat. Peninnah was jealous about how much Elkanah clearly loved Hannah, so she would continue to say cruel words to her, and Hannah would end up in tears. She would get so upset that she couldn't even eat. Her stomach was twisted up in desperation and her husband was worried about her.

"Why are you crying?" he asked her. "We've got each other, isn't that better than having ten sons?"

One day, Hannah and the whole family, including Peninnah and all her children were having a meal at Shiloh and it was clear that Hannah had really had enough of Peninnah being so evil and bitchy to her, so she stood up, left the meal and decided to go and pray to God at the temple.

Eli was the priest and he was sitting on a chair by the door, watching Hannah as she covered her face and cried deep, chest-wrenching tears of despair. He couldn't hear what Hannah was saying, he just watched her because he thought that she was behaving like a drunken wench and he was protecting the Lords temple.

Hannah prayed, "O Lord Almighty, please remember me your servant. I'm so miserable. Please give me a son and I promise that when he is old enough, I will give him back to you and he will work for you for the rest of his life. No razor will ever cut his hair."

She kept on praying silently, pouring out her heart to the Lord and Eli the priest could see her lips moving and he was cross that a drunk woman would be anywhere near the Temple of the Lord so he told her to leave and to get rid of her wine.

Hannah pulled herself to together and explained that she wasn't drunk, she was just upset and she was praying to the Lord to help her. "I've been praying to the Lord, because I am grief stricken and desperate," she sobbed.

Eli took pity on Hannah and he could see that she was genuinely seeking God so he said to her, "Go in peace, and may God answer your prayers."

Hannah thanked Eli, and returned to where the rest of the family were staying, with a smile on her face and a renewed sense of hope that something was going to change in her life. Early the next morning, everyone got up ready to go back to their home in Ramah, they worshipped God before they left, and when Elkanah and Hannah slept together, the Lord remembered Hannah's prayer and in due course she gave birth to a son whom she named Samuel which means, 'Because I asked the Lord for him'.

The next time Elkanah and the family were due to go off and make the sacrifices at Shiloh, Hannah asked Elkanah if she could stay at home because Samuel was only little and she wanted to make sure that he was weaned, and ready to be left behind, as she had promised, to work in the temple with Eli, and to serve God for the rest of his life. Elkanah agreed, and just before he left, he turned to his wife, whom he loved very much and said, "I hope God gives you the strength to keep your promise," then he left to go to Shiloh with the rest of the family.

As soon as Samuel was weaned, Hannah travelled back to Shiloh to the Temple and they took a bull with them as a sacrifice, some flour and a skin of wine and arrived at the temple to speak to Eli.

Hannah explained who she was and what promise she had made to the Lord, so Eli accepted him as a servant in the temple and then she prayed and thanked God for his blessing on her life and for delivering her from her enemies, then she returned home with Elkanah.

Samuel worked in the temple with Eli and every year Hannah would visit him and bring him new clothes as he grew bigger and bigger, when they came for their annual sacrifice. Eli prayed for Elkanah and Hannah that God would bless them with more children to replace the child that they had given to him, and in time Hannah was blessed with more children. She had three sons and two daughters.

*****

It's important to know that the book of Samuel is primarily about the first two kings of Israel, Saul and David, but it's interesting that God had decided to tell us about Samuel's birth rather than Saul and David's, so clearly it's very important. Samuel played a key role in the lives of Saul and David, he was a prophet and an anointer, so it follows that it was very important that he was born in God's timing.

Hannah not only had to put up with childlessness, but she also had to put up with a second woman in her husband's life. It was commonplace to have more than one wife, and polygamy was widely practised, even by Godly men, but it wasn't God's original plan. Right back in Genesis 2 v 24, it says,

'For this reason, a man will leave his father and mother and become united to his wife, and they will become one flesh.'

Men were supposed to be with one woman, not two, three, four or even more, and as we all know, if you have a number of women in one household, hormones start flying around and suddenly, usually nice, calm, loving women can suddenly turn into spiteful, jealous, raving cats, who all want the top position of chief wife.

Back in Hannah's day, if you didn't have children, then it was seen as shameful and God's judgement on you because of sexual immorality, so Peninnah probably thought that she had every right to be a bitch to Hannah and torment her like she did because in her eyes, Hannah must have done something wrong to be childless. Hannah would have been a social outcast, and other women in Peninnah's social circle would have excluded her from parties and other social events that they were organising. Her life would have been more miserable, and more lonely than we can really comprehend. She would have kept a low profile in the family, so as not to humiliate Elkanah in front of his male friends, but the lovely thing about this story is that Elkanah loved Hannah regardless of whether she had children or not. He didn't love her because she had given him children, he loved her for her.

That was something that I struggled to accept. I couldn't understand how I would have a long and happy marriage without children. That somehow Jon wouldn't love me quite as much, if I didn't give him a baby. That I would damage his reputation as a man, if I didn't hurry up and conceive his child. But there were countless times when Jon told me that he wanted me, whether we had children or not and I know that without Jon's continual love, back-up and support, I wouldn't have kept going.

So Elkanah loved Hannah and felt sorry for her, which made Peninnah jealous and angry, so things in their household was constantly fraught. Elkanah would have known that Peninnah was giving Hannah a hard time, and I'm sure they would have argued about it. Peninnah probably felt justified in her treatment of Hannah. Society told Peninnah that she had every right to look down upon Hannah. After all, Hannah's sin had brought this infertility upon her. Maybe she thought that kicking her out of the family house, would remove the shame from her family and protect her husband's reputation, but unfortunately for Peninnah, Elkanah loved Hannah, and he kept supporting her and loving her, never giving up on the hope that they would have a child together one day.

A good modern day analogy could be 'the ex-wife'. If your husband has been married before and has children with his former wife, and you and he are struggling to have children together, then you can probably relate to Hannah's desperation. Every time you see your husband's children, it's like your inability to have children is being constantly rubbed in your face. Imagine if your husband's ex, continually called you names and referred to you as 'unfeminine and barren' in front of other people, and what if her friends laughed at you when you were shopping in Tesco's and made jibes behind your back? Can you imagine how you would feel, being publicly humiliated like that? What if the ex-wife put horrible comments on your Facebook wall for everyone to see, or tweeted that you were sexually immoral and had caught something nasty which had made you infertile? No wonder Hannah didn't feel like eating and she cried all the time.

So how can Hannah help us?

Well, she did two vital things. In my NIV study bible, verse nine of chapter one says, 'Hannah stood up.' Three simple words, but put them in context and you'll get what I'm trying to tell you. Everyone was sitting around having a meal. Her husband was there chatting away to his friends, Peninnah was there with her friends, laughing, joking, probably making snide comments about Hannah to her friends and "**Hannah stood up**". I can imagine her glaring at Peninnah and putting her hands on her hips. She'd had enough!

Firstly, she made a decision.

She knew that there was only one answer to her nightmare existence……. God, and she needed to speak to him urgently, so she ducked out of dinner and headed up to the temple and of course the rest you've already read.

Secondly, Hannah prayed in her heart.

The pain that she was feeling, we can all relate to. It burns through your chest and becomes like a stranglehold. No wonder she couldn't eat. But Hannah spoke to God from her heart and that's a completely different type of prayer, than one that comes from your head. Your head and your heart are often in conflict. Your head is sensible, rational, cautious and questioning. It likes order and words that sound right.

Have you ever planned a prayer that you intend to speak aloud in a prayer meeting or in a church service, before you even pray it, just so that you don't say anything strange or wrong in front of everyone else?

Why? Because you don't want to forget anything? Because you want to make sure you sound spiritual enough in front of people?

When you pray from your heart, it connects directly with God and bypasses the common sense in your head. Your heart has its own language, and words that seem jumbled and desperate to you, are heard as heartfelt and real to a God that understands and loves you. Even when you can't find the words to express the devastation of childlessness to him, he knows. Even if you just groaned and whispered, "God help me," he'd understand your groan.

Often our heads or minds can come up with a lot of barriers and boundaries, that inhibit our prayer. Our minds often suggest things that are not from God, and worries and doubts that we are praying again about the same issue and the outcome is going to be the same, come creeping into our prayers and mess things up. Unbelief is not of God, so when you pray with unbelief running around in your mind, it's a waste of time. Try to bypass sensible, rational you and pray straight from your heart.

What else can Hannah's story show us?

The biggest part of Hannah's story is that Samuel was born in God's timing. I don't know anyone that enjoys waiting. God's timing and our timing never seem to match up. We want a baby at a certain time for all kinds of reasons. It might fit into our 'life' plan, we might want to be a mother before we turn forty, we might want to have a child at the same time as our friend who happens to be pregnant, we might want to have a child because our parents are pushing us for grandchildren or we might want to have a baby before Christmas because it would just be nice, but God's children are born on purpose. You have a destiny and so does your child. Don't you think God has planned their lives as well as yours?

Waiting is a hardship, and believing that God is going to answer your prayer, is even harder when the wait has been long, however, Hannah persevered in prayer. She waited years. She put up with heartache, humiliation and torment, and one day she finally got her break through.

Sarai

The story of Abraham and Sarah is huge, and I'm only going to cover a small section of the story here because it's too vast to cover in this book. There are several things that we can learn from Sarai's story, so I'll retell this in my way again, but you can read it for yourself too, if you want in Genesis 15.

We read that God made a covenant with Abram telling him that he was going to be blessed. But Abram was really disappointed that he didn't have a son, and he asked God what the point was in having blessings when he had no heir who would inherit on his death. Abram was expecting to pass everything that he owned to one of his servants, as was customary for people who had no heirs, but God told him that he would not leave everything to a servant, but that he would have a son, born to him. Then He took Abram out into the night and told him to look up into the heavens at the stars.

"Look up into the heavens and count the stars, if you can. Your descendants will be like that- too many to count." (Verse 5)

So time went on and Sarai still didn't have any children, but she knew that Abram desperately wanted a son, so she decided to work things out herself. She had a servant called Hagar, who was Egyptian, and she decided that because God had stopped her from having children, perhaps this woman Hagar could have children for her, and then they could become her children with Abram. Abram agreed, he had sex with Hagar, and she became pregnant, but unfortunately, Hagar started to look down on Sarai, even though she was her mistress, because she had managed to get pregnant, which was something that Sarai had not managed to do. Sarai got all upset about the situation, regretted her actions and then blamed Abram for having sex with Hagar, even though it was her suggestion. Sarai became very jealous, and Hagar was gloating and revelling in the new found power that she now had, so Abram had a problem on his hands. Unfortunately for Hagar, he decided to let his jealous wife, deal with her servant as she saw fit, and things went from bad to worse.

Sarai was horrible to Hagar, and treated her so badly that eventually Hagar ran away. When Hagar was on the run, she was visited by an Angel who told her that God knew all about her terrible treatment from Sarai, but that she was to return to her home, submit to her mistress and told her that she was carrying a boy who should be named Ishmael.

And so Hagar returned home, submitted to Sarai's authority and in time she gave birth to Ishmael. So Abram was eighty-six years old when he became a father for the first time.

Jump forward some thirteen years later, when Abram was ninety –nine, and he was visited by God again and reminded of the covenant that he had made with him regarding his descendants, and it is at this point that God renames Abram, and calls him Abraham because his new name means father of many nations. Abraham accepts the covenant between him and God, and every male is circumcised, as a sign of their submission and obedience to God. God also informs Abraham that his wife is to be renamed Sarah, which means princess, and that he is going to bless her and finally, she is going to have a child.

Abraham laughs because he is a very old man, and Sarah is ninety and well past childbearing age, but God is patient with Abraham, and he tells him Sarah will have a son, and that they are to call him Isaac. So Abraham puts his trust in God, and that day, he takes his thirteen year old son Ishmael, and all the males of his household, and he circumcises all of them as God has told him to do.

Some time later, three men visit with Abraham, and Abraham invites them to stay and eat with him. They cook up lots of fine food and sit underneath some nearby trees together, and one of the men asks Abraham where his wife is, to which he replies that she is inside the tent. The man then goes on to tell Abraham that in a year's time, he will visit with Abraham again, by which time Sarah will have a baby. Unbeknown to Abraham, Sarah is listening to their conversation in the tent and she hears what the man says about a baby, and she laughs at the ridiculousness of it, remarking that she is old, and worn out and

Abraham is much too old too. God hears Sarah laughing and he asks Abraham why his wife is laughing.

"Is anything too hard for the Lord........." (18 v14)

But Sarah suddenly becomes afraid of the Lord and she lies to Abraham and tells him that she wasn't laughing at all, but Abraham knows she was lying.

Time skips on and we read about the birth of Isaac in chapter 21.

'Then the Lord did exactly what he had promised. Sarah became pregnant and she gave a son to Abraham in his old age. It all happened at a time God said it would.'

He was named Isaac, which means 'he laughs', and he was circumcised at eight days old, according to the agreement that Abraham had with God.

Verse 6 is one of my favourites because you can really identify with Sarah as she says, "God has brought me laughter! All who hear about this will laugh with me. For who would have dreamed that I would ever have a baby? Yet I have given Abraham a son in his old age."

Had Sarah forgotten that she was old too?

So here are a few points that I wanted to pull out from this story.

Regardless of the fact that she is a biblical character that is long gone, she was as female and as desperate to have a baby as any modern day woman. Her childlessness lasted for decades, and it is not surprising that her first reaction to hearing that she was going to have a child at ninety, was to laugh. She was very old. In Chapter 18 v11, it says that not only was she old, but she was past her childbearing years. I'm assuming that her periods had stopped and she was no longer capable of having children naturally. The only way Sarah was going to have a child was by a divine miracle of God.

Foolishly, Sarah tried to make things happen herself, and it caused her a lot of pain and anguish. She took Hagar to Abraham, and that night, when she knew her husband was having sex with another woman, she must have laid in her bed, with all kinds of pictures going around in her head and cried in jealous anguish. But the desire to have a family with Abraham, was worth the heartbreak, or so she thought. We know that it backfired on her because Hagar got pregnant, and then gloated about it, causing Sarah more pain. There were lots of arguments, jealousy and distress. Abraham couldn't cope with it so he passed the problem straight back to a very jealous and bitter Sarah, who promptly made Hagar's life a misery. Everything was screwed up, people got hurt, no one was living in peace and nothing was going well with them, because Sarah and Abraham took matters into their own hands and tried to play God.

My grandmother used to say, "Just because you can, doesn't mean to say you should."

When my husband and I were discussing fertility treatment and how far we were prepared to take things in order to get the child we so desperately wanted, we both agreed that we did not want to use someone else's eggs, or someone else's sperm. Either of those options would mean that it wasn't wholly our biological child, so just because we could have used another woman's egg, and Jon's sperm, then implanted the embryo into my womb, didn't mean to say that it was the right thing to do. Just because it was an option, didn't make it the right option for us.

We wouldn't have wanted a woman to carry Jon's child either, if say for example I had been born without a womb. We wanted a child that was made between the two of us, or not at all, and we wanted God's blessing or not at all. It's a personal choice and one you will have to make for yourselves, but we didn't have the 'a child at any cost', attitude.

The main point in this story for me is Sarah's age. She was old and past it. Some of us who reach the big 4 0, start to panic. If you look up having a child in your forties on the internet, which incidentally I do not recommend, it is not encouraging.

BUT….. and this is a huge '*but*' for a reason, God intended for this story to be told. Sarah is not the only 'old woman' who had a child in the bible. Elizabeth, who was John the Baptist's mother, was also considered well past her sell by date. So what is God saying through this?

Have you left it too late? No. It is all in God's perfect timing. God is able to do more than we could possibly ask or imagine. In Ephesians 3 v 20-21 we read:

> God can do anything, you know—far more than you could ever imagine or guess or request in your wildest dreams! He does it not by pushing us around, but by working within us, his Spirit deeply and gently within us. Glory to God in the church! Glory to God in the Messiah, in Jesus! Glory down all the generations! Glory through all millennia! Oh, yes! (The Message)

Who told you that you were too old? Who have you been listening to?

Was Sarah really ninety when she had a baby? Wasn't age in the bible measured differently to how it is measured now? No. I think that her age is in the bible on purpose too. It could have just said, Sarah was really old, but it gives her age, and that's not incidental, so whatever you believe, the fact remains that it clearly says she was old and past childbearing age, so conceiving a child naturally was not an option for her, yet God still kept his promise to her.

I think one of the reasons why Sarah lied about her laughter, was because she was suddenly struck with the knowledge of how mighty God still was and she sensed a renewed fear of the Lord, something that she hadn't taken much notice of for many years. She began to believe the words spoken over her life were true and that she needed to take them seriously. I think the years had made her cynical, tired, disillusioned and sceptical and she had lost the relationship that she had with God. We can all become like that. We get into a habit of going to church every Sunday, or when we feel like it, and we sing and pray, hoping month after month for our miracle and when God doesn't come up with the answer, we turn our backs, leave the church and stop praying and in some weird way, think we are punishing God because he won't give us our baby. But really all we are doing is harming ourselves by cutting ourselves off from God. It's exactly what the enemy wants. When we stand alone, trying to work out our own problems in our own way, we are easy pickings, and the enemy can swoop in, and make mincemeat out of us. You'll start believing every lie he can get you to read, watch on TV, or upload onto your computer.

I think that is the same for many people who are waiting for God's promises to be fulfilled in their lives. People run out of hope, and then they lose the knowledge of the awesomeness of God and it's not until someone speaks into your life, plugs you back into God once more and wakes you up to the truth, that you begin to see that your God has not abandoned you, that he is still holding you and he knows all about you.

Rebekah

This is another complicated story with lots of relatives and brothers and servants, which you can read in Genesis 25. So in a nutshell, Sarah died, and left Abraham behind and he was concerned that his son Isaac wasn't married yet. Abraham was getting on in years and wanted things to be settled for his son before he died too. He wanted Isaac to marry a nice girl from his homeland, so he asked his servant to go off and find a suitable bride. Not an easy task, especially when the groom isn't going along with you, and you have to use your own judgment on the type of woman he might like. So Abraham says to the servant, 'Look, stop worrying. I know Isaac isn't coming with you to help choose his wife, so what I'll do is, I'll ask God to send an Angel on ahead, and make sure that you meet the right woman." Simple.

So the poor servant had the unenviable task of finding the right girl for his master's son. He sets off with ten camels that are packed with expensive gifts to impress the future wife of his master's son, and arrives in Aram-Naharaim, which is where Abraham's brother Nahor has set up home. He arrives at the town well, right at the time when the local women are coming out to fill up their water jugs and he prays to God and says, 'there are lots of women here and I want to get the right one, so

I'll ask one for a drink and if she offers to water all ten camels too, then I'll know it's her."

Sure enough, a very beautiful young woman approaches the well and the servant thinks, 'she's nice, I'll try her first,' and he asks her for a drink. Not only does she give him a drink, but she offers to water the camels too. He waits to see if she'll do all ten camels, and when she does, he knows that he's found the right girl. He gives her a gold ring for her nose and a couple of large gold bracelets for her wrists, just to prove that he's carrying a message from someone wealthy and important and asks the girl who her family are, and if they could put him up overnight.

They head back to her family home, and the servant is delighted to find out that she is a distant relative and perfect for Isaac. Her family seems very impressed with the gifts and agree to let Rebekah marry Isaac. The following morning, Rebekah's family are a little bit reticent about letting their lovely daughter travel such a long way from home, so they ask if she can stay at home for a little while longer, but the servant is keen to get back. Rebekah is summoned by her family and asked if she is happy to leave, and she agrees, so off they go.

When they are almost back to the land where Abraham and Isaac live, in the distance, Isaac sees the camels approaching and he knows that the servant is on his way back and he's curious to see who he has picked out as his wife. He runs across the fields to meet them and Rebekah sees him coming and asks the servant who it is and is informed that it is his master. Rebekah gets off her mount, covers her face with her veil and meets her future husband for the first time. Ah, romance.

Isaac meets Rebekah, is pleased with the servant's choice and listens to how he chose her, and then he takes her back to his mother's tent, marries her and loves her very much because she is a comfort to him after his mother's death.

Moving on to Genesis 25 v 19, we see that Isaac and Rebekah married when Isaac was forty, but there were no children born in the marriage until Isaac pleaded with God for Rebekah to have a child because she was childless. God heard him and she conceived twins. Esau and Jacob weren't born until Isaac was sixty.

Isaac and Rebekah would have prayed for years and years to have children and finally their prayer was answered after twenty years, but it is interesting that we read of the husband praying to the Lord this time, rather than the woman pleading for God to intervene.

Often other people forget how much pressure the man is under when it comes to childlessness. Lots of people can sympathise with the woman, and understand her disappointment and frustration, but what about the man?

I know that a lot of men feel like a failure when they can't get their wife pregnant. There is something very masculine and primal about being a father, and proving to the other males that they are capable, Alpha male types. Men aren't supposed to break down in floods of tears in front of everyone on the football pitch because their wife has just started her period again, and men don't tend to get together for coffee and chocolate muffins to talk about ovulation and cramping. Childlessness is often seen as a female problem because we're the ones with the desperate maternal instinct, but male paternal instinct needs to be addressed to.

Isaac pleaded with God, on his wife's behalf *and* because he wanted children desperately himself. His cry was heartfelt, just like Hannah. Neither of them would have known who's fault it was, because they didn't have tests like that, but the humiliation and disgrace to his family name would have been hard to live with. People would have been gossiping, and making all kinds of judgments about him as a man, and his ability to lead his family like his father before him, and I bet a few thought that he should have married a nice Canaanite girl and not bothered going all the way across the country for some 'slip of a thing', that couldn't get pregnant. It would have been a living nightmare for him, and Rebekah, but he loved her, and prayed to God himself.

If the reason for your childlessness, is due to your husband, then suggests he talks not just to you, but to other men who are reliable, confidential and can support him. You may have female friends to talk to and confide in, but they need someone outside of the situation to talk to and pray with, too. Lots of men don't confide in others because it's thought of as a weakness and confiding about something that affects their maleness, is like a double whammy.

Try to be reassuring, even if you are heartbroken about the situation. I hope you chose him because you loved him, not for what he could give you.

And finally, it doesn't matter who's got the problem, whether it's you or him, or both of you, God's name is higher than every infertility name that the doctors can come up with.

Leah and Rachel

I'm exhausted after reading this story. They pop out one baby after another, scream and shout at each other, and cry and wail at their husband Jacob, (one of the twins born to Isaac and Rebekah), and between them they drive him nuts so that he ends up shouting, 'Am I God? He is the only one to give you children!" Poor man. I wonder if he ever hid in the potting shed?

You can read the story in Genesis 29 onwards. The whole marriage to both women is a mess and everyone is deceiving each other. Jacob really fancies Rachel because she's gorgeous and has a lovely figure and her dad, Laban agrees to let Jacob marry her, and they have this big old wedding, he takes her to his bed, and when he wakes up in the morning….. ta dah!.... it's her sister Leah instead of the lovely Rachel. Jacob isn't very impressed because part of the deal to marry Rachel was that he would have to work for Laban for seven years and he can't get out of it now. So anyway, Laban says that it's not his custom to marry the youngest daughter off first before the oldest daughter is wed, but if he still wants Rachel then he's going to have to work for another seven years. Jacob says that he wants Rachel, and agrees to work for another seven years, and only a week later, he marries Leah's sister, takes her to his bed, and big,

big problems start happening between the two sisters, because Jacob loves Rachel and not Leah.

God sees that Leah is unloved, so he blesses her with the first child, and the second child, and the third and they are all boys which is what every man really wants. Leah thinks that Jacob is going to love her now, but Rachel is still his favourite. Rachel starts to get very jealous of her sister and is desperate to have a child with Jacob too. This is when she cries at Jacob and begs him for a child, and Jacob tells her that only God can give her a child.

One day, Leah's oldest son Reuben is working on the fields and he finds some mandrake plants growing, so he digs them up and brings the roots to his mother. Rachel sees that Leah has mandrake roots, and she begs her sister for some because it was widely believed that the mandrake root helped with infertility.

Leah gets cross and says, ' You took my husband and now you want my sons mandrake roots?" But Rachel begs her and says that if she will let her have the roots, she will let Jacob sleep with her tonight." Leah agrees and walks out to the fields at the end of the day when Jacob is on his way back to Rachel, meets up with him and tells him that she has just 'bought him' for the night with the mandrake roots. So Jacob goes home with Leah for the night, and she gets pregnant again.

The women are in a constant battle to produce as many sons as they can, and they even offer their servants to have children with Jacob, so now Jacob is sleeping with even more women and getting them pregnant too! After Leah had given birth to six sons, and one daughter, and the servants had produced babies for Jacob too, God remembered Rachel's plight, and answered her prayers.

She gave birth to Joseph, saying, 'God has removed my shame' and later on in the story we hear that she also had a son called Benjamin, but sadly she died in childbirth when he was born.

So the main points in this story for me are that nothing started well. The girls were sisters, and they were continually trying to outdo each other all the time. Their household must have been full of strife. Leah was hurt that she was unloved, and that her husband had married her younger, prettier sister only a week after marrying her, and she felt ugly, worthless and let down.

Rachel was younger, prettier and loved by Jacob. She was his first choice, and she would have watched her older sister marry the man that she loved, and resentment would have built in her heart. To share your husband with another woman would have been hard work anyway, but to have to share him with your sister would have been a nightmare. The constant need to prove yourself better than her, would have been overwhelming. And being unable to have a child, would have made Rachel feel worthless and unfeminine. She had to watch her sister have seven children, and two servants gave Jacob four more children and still she was childless. No wonder she cried out.

Rachel decides to take matters into her own hands when she finds out that her nephew Reuben has got some mandrake roots and they are reported to be the miracle fertility drug that she needs. She's going to get herself pregnant and she is so determined that this is going to work this time, that she *lets Jacob* sleep with Leah. It's interesting that Jacob doesn't seem to have much say in the matter. Rachel *lets* him have sex, and Leah *tells* him to have sex, so he just does as he's told? Perhaps he just can't cope with the hassle anymore and wants to keep everyone happy?

You know, sometimes, as desperate mums-to-be, we can be a nightmare to live with. We *make* our husbands have sex with us at certain times of the month and they *have* to take their vitamins, they *have* to keep their jiggly bits cool and they *can't* soak in a nice hot bath. They *can't* drink alcohol, or have a cigar after dinner. They *have* to be patient when we're stressed out, they *have* to drink green tea and not thick, black coffee with too much caffeine. And then, when they've done all that, and we're still not pregnant, they *have* to be cried on, they *have* to go out and buy vast quantities of chocolate and then they *have* to start again next month.

What's attractive about that? Maybe Jacob thought great, I'll sleep with Leah because Rachel's been going on and on at me for a child for months now. Maybe it wasn't such a hardship sleeping with a couple of willing servants too. At least it was a change from a whinging wife.

Being demanding, bossy, whiny and needy, isn't going to do much for your sex life. Remember when you had sex because you fancied each other and couldn't wait to jump each others bones? Remember when making love was unrushed and it didn't matter if you didn't do it in a certain position, you just loved each other? What about when you had no idea what time of the month it was and you were making love just because you wanted to?

If you've lost that, then back up, reverse, and try and get the foundation stones in place first or you'll lose a vital ingredient in your life…… your marriage.

Trying for a baby is up there on the 'stress list' amongst good old favourites like moving house, starting a new job, bankruptcy, death and divorce.

If you are a Christian, and trying for a baby is stressing you out to the point where you only have sex when you're ovulating, and your whole life depends on whether you have a child or not, then I would suggest that you are doing it all in your own strength without God, and you need to stop.

Ask yourself what comes first and what is driving your life, and if your answer is having a baby, you've got a problem.

God should be first. Your relationship with him will carry you through everything, and you know this really, you've just got to a point where you actually can't cope and you are refusing to hand it over to God. You've tried everything and you are all prayed out, but what that really means is that you are all, 'you'd out', and you feel like a failure.

I've prayed!

God isn't listening to me!

Why do fifteen year olds get pregnant and not me?

Why her and not me?

Eat this, drink that, don't do this, don't do that.

We *have* to do it tonight!

Come home from work early, I'm ovulating! Yes, now!

God never intended for your life to be filled with strife. It is not God's will for you. He created you to have a relationship with him; a personal, loving, interactive relationship. Sometimes we need to go back to the start, and reassess what went wrong, and why God is no longer the focal point, and the joy in our hearts, and has become more like the last resort, and the one to blame for our problems. Understanding our value to God, and learning to rest in his presence, when all our hopes seem to be

crumbling around us, will allow peace back in our lives. God
never planned for us to trudge this road alone.

You need to come to the end of doing it all yourself and
be peaceful and still enough in your heart to hear God
whispering that he knows you are devastated.

Abortion

I told you earlier in this book about my friend that had an abortion after she and her boyfriend decided that they didn't want to have a child together. I explained how it affected me and how I begged her to let me have the child. I offered to financially help her, to buy her clothes, and she could have moved in to live with us too, but that was me acting in desperation, and really I knew in my heart of hearts that she wouldn't go for that.

I have spoken to several women over the years who have had abortions and all of them regret it. I know that for some women that is not the case, but I haven't met anyone like that, so I'm just talking from my experience.

I believe that having an abortion is fundamentally wrong and is unnecessary if the mother and the child are both well and healthy. I can understand a woman terminating a pregnancy if her life is at risk, or if the pregnant female is very, very young, say of primary school age, for example, but I think that abortion is more harmful to the woman, than actually having the baby and giving the child up for adoption. Both options hurt, but in my opinion, adoption hurts less. You are choosing life for your child and a life with someone that will be able to care for them, and surely that is better than ending their life completely.

But as Christians, it's not our job to judge anyone. A number of my friends have had terminations, and I love my friends and no one, including me, has got a perfect life or knows everything. It is their business, they made the decision at a time in their lives when things were awful. My job is to love them, support them and be a friend.

If you have had an abortion and you are struggling to come to terms with what happened, speak to someone you trust. Talk and talk, until you are talked out and feel that you have shared enough to be able to get some peace about the situation, then try and move on. I believe that God can forgive you wholeheartedly and make your life whole again. God does not want you to suffer or do some kind of penance for your sins, his son Jesus died once, for everyone, for everything that we have ever done, and if you ask him to forgive you once, that's it. You don't have to keep dragging up all your old stuff. There is a prayer at the end of the book if you want to follow something yourself.

If you have had an abortion and you have brought this time in your life before God, and have said sorry, but now you are struggling to get pregnant, God is not punishing you because you had an abortion. I believe that so strongly, I'm going to say it again. Ready?

God is not punishing you because you had an abortion.

Read it again, and swallow it, because it's true. God does not hold onto your sins in a big book and make you suffer because of them. If you think that, then you really don't know

God, and perhaps you should make an appointment to speak to him, so that you understand who you are praying to.

If you, GOD, kept records on wrongdoings,
  who would stand a chance?
As it turns out, forgiveness is your habit,   and
that's why you're worshipped.

Psalm 130 v 3 The Message.

Miscarriage, still birth and early childhood death

It doesn't matter if you were six weeks pregnant when you miscarried and your baby didn't even look human, it was still a real person with your DNA and your personality traits. The child had a soul from the moment of conception and it was a real human being whom God knew before conception.

I believe that every child that dies, goes to be with Jesus in heaven, regardless of their parents religious beliefs. I believe that Angels come and escort those little human soul to heaven and they grow up and live with Jesus.

I am convinced that one day when I die, and I go to heaven to be with Jesus, that I will meet my child who died because of an ectopic pregnancy. I think I may have had at least one other miscarriage as well, but I can't be sure on that, however, if that is the case, then that child is there with Jesus too, and they are waiting to meet their parents and their other siblings one day.

You might think I'm nuts, but Jesus is a winner of souls. Age has nothing to do with anything. If a soul is a few days old or decades old, Jesus died for all and every soul is precious to him. When I watch the news and I hear that a child has died somehow, maybe in a house fire or a car accident, I know in my heart, that they are with Jesus, instantaneously and that they are waiting for their parents to join them one day.

Read, 'Heaven is for Real', by Todd Burpo, it's awesome and it confirms everything that my heart already believes is true. It means that the relationship you never had with your child, is still going to happen, because nothing is lost. Your child is temporarily growing up somewhere else, with Jesus and they are safe, happy and loved. If you are a Christian and believe in God, you will see them again.

Fertility treatment

This is something that you have to talk about together as a couple. Pray together, and make the decision together, but don't be rushed. If you needed medical assistance because you'd broken your leg, then you probably wouldn't think twice about putting your leg in plaster, and if you needed antibiotics for an infection, you'd go and get your prescription filled, so if you need straightforward medical assistance because you have blocked tubes or your hormone levels are wonky, then go for it. It doesn't show a lack of faith by using medical intervention. I believe that God can use the doctors to answer prayer, and to heal people too. We're blessed to have modern hospitals.

If you want to try IVF, then this is your decision too, providing you both understand everything that is involved and you both want to go ahead and do it.

The only reason Jon and I didn't go for IVF, was because we didn't want to use someone else's egg or sperm. For us, we wanted to have a child that was genetically ours. If we had been able to use my eggs and Jon's sperm, and we could have afforded it, then we would have considered IVF.

The only reservation I have with IVF is when it is used for genetic screening. I believe that this is ethically wrong, and only selecting healthy eggs to implant and disregarding all the others is in my opinion also morally wrong. I believe that a human person is created at the moment of conception, when the egg and sperm start dividing into cells. Flushing away eggs that are not 'perfect', in my opinion, devalues human life.

Storing eggs that have been fertilised is also a tricky subject. I would want to give each embryo the chance of life, and therefore if I couldn't physically carry anymore children myself, I would donate them to another couple rather than have their lives wasted.

Surrogacy is a wonderful thing to do for someone else, but it does have its issues as well. Think about how you are going to explain to your child, that his grandma is actually his tummy mummy, and that you are also his sister as well as his mummy. Just because you can, doesn't mean to say you should. Think about the bigger picture before you undertake anything like this. Go and get some really good counselling from people who know what they are talking about, and that might not necessarily be your church pastor. Speak to people with experience in this area. Pray and ask God to direct your path and wait for him to give you the green light before you proceed with something like this.

Taking medications and fertility drugs is fine in my opinion, but I think the most important aspect of this section is to make your own decision and be peaceful before God about it. Don't rush anything. Pray first.

Adoption

There are hundreds and hundreds of children who are desperate for a 'Forever Family.'

I am a member of an adoption panel and I help to interview potential adoptive parents and match them with children looking for families. It's a great job, but sometimes it can be frustrating. If you are going to adopt, stick with it. See it through and go on the training courses. Don't think you know it all. Go and learn about the types of children that need families and what they are likely to be like, and consider an older child because they always get left behind. Everyone wants the cute baby, but not many will take a little boy who is five and has had a tough life already. Think about it seriously, pray about it all the time, and if God says yes, then go for it wholeheartedly and be the best parent you can be, as an act of worship to God.

You don't have to be married to adopt, you can be a single parent. You don't have to own your own house, you can be in a rented place. You don't have to be rich, you have to be generous. You have to like children, (which might surprise you), but some people only adopt because they think that's the accepted norm in society. You don't have to be a parent to be socially acceptable. If it's not for you, then it's not for you. You have to have time, love, empathy and respect. And finally, you have to be able to parent someone else's birth child and love them unconditionally, forever, and those people are very special.

Putting God First

My final challenge is this. Does God come first in your life? Don't jump to say yes immediately,….. think about it.

Does he come first? Do you have any time for God in your life?

It's important to put the foundation of the building right before you start to build on them. Get yourself a notebook, any notebook will do or a posh journal, I don't mind, but something that you can keep just for you and God. Set aside time every day to read from the bible, pray to God and listen to him. Start off realistically, say twenty minutes. Try and find some regular daily bible reading, for example the UCB daily readings are available online. You can listen to someone read it to you or you can read it for yourself, but either way, allow God to speak to you each day. Write down anything that stands out, anything that you think God might be highlighting, make sure that you date the entry so that you can remember when you read it, and then write down what you are going to pray about. My journal usually looks a little like this:

UCB 3rd Feb 2013.

Mark 9 v 23-24 'I do believe – but help me not to doubt! Praying for Jon, kids, finances, and dog's itchy face.

Over the course of a few weeks, you'll see that God is talking to you through the daily readings and every day is an encouragement to keep going. Sometimes the reading will be random and you'll wonder what you are going to receive from God today, but if you allow yourself to quieten down, and let God speak, you'll be amazed at what new things he can reveal to you about your life, and what he thinks about you. It will make God the focus of your life, and not the constant burden of making a baby. God needs to be your focus because without him, you are lost, but with him, all things are possible.

Jesus looked hard at them and said, "No chance at all if you think you can pull it off yourself. Every chance in the world if you trust God to do it."

Matt 19 v26. The Message.

In conclusion

There are no rules that say you have to have children, or anywhere in the bible that says you've got to have a family otherwise God won't be pleased with you. What is the right decision for one couple, might not be right for another, but both are equally important and valid. I have a number of friends who have chosen not to have children, and they are happy with their decision, and contented with the life that God has given to them. Their lives are packed with projects and other work opportunities that God has specifically given them, and they don't see themselves as unfulfilled in any way, and neither do I. I also have a number of friends who have finished trying for a family, and have either gone down the adoption route, or have decided that children are not for them after all. Some of them have taken a long time to accept this, but all of them are now in a place where they feel that they can breathe because the strain and expectations, often from other people, is no longer there.

People with children are not more blessed than those who don't have any, whether through choice, or circumstance. The most important aspect of all of this is to know what God's calling is in your life, and understand who you are in Christ, not what you hoped you would be.

However, I believe that if you want a family, then there is no reason why you can't have one, and I knew that this was what God wanted for me. You've read that my life, even as a little girl, was all about having children, so I believe that God placed that desire in my heart, and gave me the determination to keep going.

If you don't get pregnant, but you decide to adopt, then that's fantastic. Adoption is not a second rate option to having your own children, nor does it say that your faith isn't strong enough to believe for a birth child, it just means that God is leading you in a different direction, and you were listening quietly, and peacefully enough to hear him speak to you.

I hope this book will be an

encouragement to you and a

blessing.

love Louise x

Suggested prayers as a guide.

A prayer of faith to ask for a baby.

Father God, Thank you for hearing all of my prayers. I know that you have been with me for my entire life, and you know all about me. Please help me to conceive a child with my husband. Please heal anything in my body that isn't working correctly because you made me in the first place, and only you can put this right. Please help me to believe and not doubt, and please help me to overcome fear and worry that stops me from receiving your best for my life. Please give me an easy pregnancy, and an easy birth, and bless this child that you are giving me. I want to pray for ********* who is also trying for a baby, and I pray that you will bless them and give them a child too.

I'm asking you in the name of Jesus, Amen.

A prayer for forgiveness.

Father God, please forgive me for the abortion that I had in ******. I know that you forgive everything, and in faith I am handing this over to you because I have carried this burden for long enough now. I believe that you love me, that you have set me free from any guilt associated with this and I am a new person because you love me, and your son died for me.

In Jesus name, Amen.

A prayer for bereavement.

Father God, my heart breaks that I have lost my child.
Please give me peace in my heart, and hold me in your loving
arms. Thank you that you promise that you will never leave me
or forsake me, and that you are always with me in every
situation. Please help me today, I pray, and bring me and my
family peace.

In Jesus name, Amen.

So you're not a Christian?

I believe that if you call out to God, the creator of everything, he will hear you, even if you are not a Christian. I have prayed for many of my non Christian friends over the years, and God has heard me and answered my prayers.

We are all human, and uniquely special, and God loves everyone regardless of race, ethnicity, or culture.

If you're reading this book, then that probably means that you're in the same situation as millions of other women across the globe, and you're looking for answers. God is the only answer to your situation, and if you've tried everything you can to have a child, and you're financially devastated, as well as emotionally worn down, then perhaps it's time you handed your life over to the one that made you, and asked him to come and help you.

Coming to the end of ourselves, and handing the hurt, the pain, the disappointment and the loss over to God, who knows you intimately better than anyone else ever will, gives you a sense of peace that you can't get from anything else. You can yoga yourself to death, you can bong and chant, you can do handstands and speak to your womb demanding it get pregnant, and you can pump your body full of drugs until you bloat up and throw up, but when God sees that you have come to the end of yourself, and you are relying solely on him for your family, then he will step in and give you the peace that you have been longing for.

Families come in all different shapes. Children come into families in all different ways. Your job is to hold your arms open and love whoever comes your way.

I am not promising a baby for you. That's not my job and anyone who promises that, is not telling you the truth, but I know that hundreds of women have prayed their miracle babies into their lives, and God is waiting for you to speak to him, even if you have never done it before.

A prayer to become a Christian.

Father God, I want to give my life to you. I am sorry for all the things that I have done in my life that were sinful, and I repent of all of them. I believe that you are the only God, that your son died for me, and that I now have a new life because of Jesus. Thank you for accepting me into your family, and I pray that you will show me what to do with my life, that you will give me some Christian friends that will help me and encourage me, and that you will keep me safe and secure.

In Jesus name, Amen.

About Jon and Louise Sibley

Jon and Louise Sibley, pastor Crossroad Christian Fellowship in Seaton, Devon. They have four children, Harry, Lily, Jesse and Tom, and a mad Labradoodle called Billy Goat. Since taking over the leadership of their church in 2012, their greatest desire is to make Jesus, the centre of people's lives.

"We want to equip Christians, by providing them with help, inspiration, friendship and encouragement, so that they can fulfil their God given potential and discover what great plans God has for their lives."

Jon is a full time pastor and spends a great of time preparing teaching materials, planning services, visiting people, and being actively involved in all aspects of the church. He was a youth pastor for many years, running various children's clubs, and teenage groups, as well as a Sunday school teacher for a number of years

Louise writes, "Jon is the best. He is a fantastic husband, and father, and he is an inspirational leader. He never boasts about anything. He is quietly unassuming and humble. He cooks for me every Saturday night, and spoils me all the time. We make a point of having marriage time together because we are more than just parents, and pastors, we are best friends. Being married to your best friend is great, and he is especially good at roasting chicken!"

Jon writes, "I also do a great pork in cider sauce. Seriously though, being a husband and father is the highest calling I have. The family comes first, after all, the bible says that if a man can't look after his own family, how can he possibly look after a church (my own translation). Having said that, I am passionate about people discovering God as our Father and encouraging others into a deeper relationship with Jesus, helping them to find who they are in Christ through the power of the Spirit.

"Louise is an amazing wife and mum. She has been the inspiration behind us fostering, adopting from China and from the UK. Without her drive, God given vision and enthusiasm we would not have done any of it. She shares God's heart about the care for widows and orphans and wants to see everyone being part of a loving, stable family."

You can email Louise at: louise@crossroad.org.uk.

Lightning Source UK Ltd.
Milton Keynes UK
UKOW03f0654260314

9 780957 100718